Data Management at Work

Dr Kathy Lang is a computer systems consultant and technical writer, especially of manuals for non-specialist users. She takes a particular interest in the human factors in computer systems design, office automation and commercial applications of microcomputers.

Kathy Lang spent fourteen years of her computing career at the Universities of Newcastle and Birmingham before setting up a consultancy with her husband, Dr Terry Lang, in 1981. She is based in Looe, Cornwall.

Kathy N. Lang

Data Management at Work

A Guide for the Personal Computer User

Pan Original
Pan Books London and Sydney

First published 1985 by Pan Books Ltd,
Cavaye Place, London SW10 9PG
9 8 7 6 5 4 3 2 1
© Kathy N. Lang 1985
ISBN 0 330 28874 1

Printed and bound in Great Britain by
Richard Clay (The Chaucer Press) Ltd, Bungay, Suffolk

For Terry

Contents

Part 1
Introduction

The first part of this book is intended to introduce you to its basic ideas and approach, and to describe in detail a real situation in which great benefit could be derived from the abilities of a computer system to manage information.

1 Introduction

Once, all computer systems were large, expensive and needed a special environment in which to operate. Because they were expensive and also opaque to the ordinary person, even the smallest computer had at least a couple of technical experts to attend to its needs, and to act as go-betweens for the people who needed the computer's help in running their business. That was not always a satisfactory solution, as many of these go-betweens were much better at speaking computerese than they were at understanding business or scientific problems. Since the arrival of low-cost, reliable small computers, many people who would otherwise not have been able to afford a computer can now buy one for business, pleasure or a mixture of the two.

As a result, many people either have a computer or have the use of one, or think that a computer may be able to help them, but have no training in computing. Nor do they wish to become involved in learning about computers for their own sake. This book is for people who think that a computer may be able to help them, and who want to use the computer as a tool, without getting involved with the computer itself any more than is absolutely necessary.

This book is not, however, written to tell people what sort of computer system to buy, nor how to choose the computer system itself. This is where buying computers is quite different from buying a car, washing machine or almost any other piece of equipment, and this difference is a major reason for mistaken purchases. Once you have bought a car, your major decisions are over. To run it, all you have to do is fill it with petrol, and off you go. The petrol for computers is the software – the programs, which are simply the sets of instructions which tell the computer what to do. Choosing the right software, and applying it sensibly, is a much harder job than choosing the computer itself. It involves both deciding what functions you want to carry out, and selecting software which will best carry out those functions.

The aim of this book is to help in both these tasks. However, it is not concerned with all applications of computers, but rather with those in which the information to be processed has some inherent regularity of structure. This sort of information is frequently stored in a manual card index. However, a card index has severe limitations. The number of cards may become too large to be handled easily. Or the limitations of pieces of card for categorising may prove cumbersome. Or you may want to carry out tasks to which the card index is unsuited, such as totalling the value of an item across every card.

There are three ways such information can be handled on a computer. You can write or commission a program or suite of programs specially for the task, which is likely to prove expensive, error-prone and time-consuming. Or, if such a commodity exists, you can buy a package specially written for your particular need – Hotel Bookings, Crop Rotation, Television Rentals. Sometimes this is an appropriate route, if your problem is well defined, and there is a package to match – with good support close to you.

A third possibility is to use a general-purpose data management or data base management system. These systems are designed especially to deal with the structured information with which we are concerned here. That is, each set of items of information processed by a data management system has a common form, and is to be treated in a similar way. (An example would be records held about patients, where the doctor wishes to find out how many consultations have been held in the last three months.) The simplest data management systems are modelled on the familiar card index. The most complex and sophisticated data base management systems are capable of, say, handling 100 simultaneous requests from travel agents trying to book holidays with a major tour operator. Even on a microcomputer used by one person, the range of possibilities is enormous.

In addition, such systems can often be adapted to meet particular needs, with nearly as much flexibility as if special-purpose programs had been written. Data management systems can thus be thought of as providing most of the features which you can get with a purpose-built program, but with much less work and fewer errors. For all these reasons, the major part of this book, and of the examples used, will concentrate on this type of software.

However, one vital step must be taken first if you are planning to introduce a computer system, or even to assess whether it may be sensible to introduce a computer system. (This applies whether your needs can be met by a package, or whether you need a specially written program or a data management system adapted to your application.) At present, you see your needs in terms of how your business, department or office works. If you were asked how you thought a computer might help, you would reply in terms such as 'we want to get our invoices out faster' or 'we want tighter control over our costing methods' or 'we'd like to make it easier to carry out large mailings to customers'. Asked how this might be achieved, you are most likely to base your reply on the manual or simple mechanical methods you use at present.

A solution to your problems will not, however, be couched in terms of your application, or indeed of any real-life application, but in terms of the solution it provides. The manual which describes the computerised system will talk in terms of 'setting up a data file' and 'doing an extract and sort run', rather than describing its features in terms of your objectives. In order to choose an appropriate system, and to implement it together with some procedures suitable for your working environment, you will have to be able to bridge that gap. Your success in doing so will be a major factor in the effectiveness of your attempts to use or introduce a computer into your work.

Sometimes the situation is sufficiently complicated for this to be impossible without professional help from independent consultants. Even in that case, you are more likely to get good results if you have a clear understanding of your needs, and can bridge the gap between your objectives and the solutions which computer systems can provide. A major task of this book is to give you some help in this venture, by taking you through the stages of deciding:

- what sort of information you have;
- what you want to do with it;

- how much information you have and how often it is to be processed;
- who will process the information;
- how to choose a package appropriate to your needs;
- how to put a computerised system into use.

Throughout, the aim will be to explore your needs – the problems you want to solve – and to look at the available solutions in the light of these requirements. To help in this, particular data management systems will be used to illustrate points, but you will not find detailed instructions on using any particular package. Instead, there will be worked examples of how particular applications have been implemented, which you should be able to apply in solving your own problems. The packages used in the examples are all available on microcomputers which can run the main business operating systems (CP/M, MS-DOS and PC-DOS, for the technically minded). It should be emphasised that examples from individual packages have been selected, not necessarily because those packages are superior to others not mentioned, but because they provide particularly suitable examples of the point being illustrated.

For those who need more information about the features of individual packages, there is an appendix giving sources of additional help. At the beginning of each chapter you will find a paragraph or two summarising the basic ideas to be discussed, which will help you to organise the material you will be reading. The aim is to give you some pegs on which to hang the information which follows. This summary may also help you to see if the information is relevant to your needs: for instance, those whose requirements do not include the handling of running text may be able to ignore some parts of the book. Within the summaries, key words and phrases are printed in heavier type, to help you to identify the crucial elements in each chapter.

If you decide to use, or are already using, a computer system, you are likely to encounter a good deal of technical material which is intended to be referred to rather than read. This book has the opposite aim: of being read rather than studied, of being regarded as a book rather than as a manual. I hope you will find it so.

2 A case study

*It often helps, when trying to understand new concepts and apply them in your environment, to see **examples** of how other similar situations have been handled. So the second part of this book takes most of its examples from a **case study** of an organisation which is investigating the **potential of data management systems for solving some everyday problems**. In this chapter, the* background *to these problems is examined, to make the detailed examples clearer.*

To bridge the gap between your objectives and a possible solution to meet them, you need to begin with a statement of those objectives and needs. For example, you might find the president of a sports and social club saying something like this:

Bill is the secretary of our local social club. The club is prosperous and has several hundred members; the premises consist of a building in the town with bars and an entertainment area, and a football field and a group of tennis courts on the outskirts of the town, each with a small pavilion with a bar. At the end of the year, Bill will be retiring and handing over to a younger member. Bill has been doing the job for thirty years, knows every member by name, and can recite the current state of the membership books whenever he's asked. His successor, Ken, is not keen to emulate these feats, and thinks a computer could help him to keep the membership records straight. Another problem he would like help with is letting members with particular interests know when there is a special event on – at the moment Bill knows all this without having to write anything down.

At the back of Ken's mind is a vague idea that a computer system might help to make even more profits from the bars, by finding the best suppliers from the many available, especially at times like Christmas when there tends to be lots of quite complicated special offers. Ken's friend Donald, who organises the annual club holidays to ski and sun resorts, thinks a computer system could help to avoid the embarrassments of last year when one trip was overbooked and another lost a lot of money. I'm worried about how much it would all cost, and whether it would be worth it. Bill is very suspicious of the whole thing, and wants to know what will happen when the computer goes wrong.

This example includes several aspects often found when analysing the needs of a business, office or club for a data management system. We shall use the example both to give instances of detailed points to consider, and, in the last part of the book, to develop ideas about how a complete system could be put together. The first task, then, is to look at the example in more detail.

What's the top priority?

Faced with this kind of problem, the first thing to decide is where to begin. People usually have a strong feeling about which problem is the most urgent. In this case, the membership records system is the obvious problem, since Ken does not have Bill's encyclopaedic memory experience, and could not operate the system in the same way. This is quite a common situation in businesses and offices. There is another advantage in starting with that kind of problem: the person who will operate the new system is unlikely to be pre-judiced against it in favour of the old, familiar, inadequate manual system.

Answering this question does not mean that you should forget about other needs for the time being – far from it, as you will see later in this chapter. But you should usually investigate the most urgent application first, not only because it requires an early solution, but also because it is likely to be the most concrete.

In the example of the club membership, the manual system in use at the moment does have some written backing. This consists of a simple manual card index, containing each member's name, address and membership fee, and the date he or she joined the club. There is also an indication of whether payment has been made for the current year, and a place to enter members' particular interests – playing table-tennis or pool, going on theatre outings and so on. An example of the card appears below.

```
                    Seaside Sports and Social Club

                                              Mr A. B. Smith
Family member                                 14 Berry Road
                                              Parkway
                                              SEASIDE
                                              PL13 2HH

Joined:  13 December 1983
Annual subscription:  £20.00
Years paid:  1983

Interests:  tennis, bowls, pool, table-tennis
```

Figure 1 **Card used in manual club membership system**

These cards are started up when a member first joins – or about
then, depending on how busy the office is at the time, and on how
soon the person signing up a new member remembers to fill in the
forms. Once in the index, each card is processed at least once a year,
when the member's annual subscription is paid – this just involves
the club typist adding the current year to the list of years paid. If the
treasurer is away, someone else will check the cards looking for
members who would like to play in the table-tennis team, or who
haven't paid their subscriptions. However, with about 600
members, this can take some time.

The manual system could be improved in several ways. For
example, the cards of those who have paid their subscription for the
current year could be moved to another box, so that one box
contains all the defaulters separately from the paid-up members.
However, when this was suggested, it turned out that the club would
also like to make it possible for people to join at other times of the
year, and have their subscriptions run from the appropriate month
in that year to the same month in the next. This would make it much
easier in one way to cope with subscription renewal, since it would
reduce the volume of payments made at any one time. However, in
a manual system it would not be easy to find those members whose

subscriptions are due each month, nor to improve the system of finding members with particular interests.

The basic problem is that the club needs the information in three different forms: ordered by member name to be able to check quickly on individuals' queries, by month of joining for subscription renewal, and by interests. The last format presents a further problem, in that one member could have several interests, so ordering by one would not help to find the others.

What else is needed?

Membership records represent the club's top priority; if subscriptions could be gathered in more quickly, the club could make substantial gains in interest on those payments, which would go some way to paying for a computer. But the work would not keep the computer fully occupied all the time. (There is, of course, no reason why it should – if a computer system will save its cost in a reasonable period, or bring other benefits of comparable value, it is economic to buy it even if it is only in use for two hours each week. But since the priority application will not use the computer system full-time, the club has the **opportunity** to use it for other tasks.) Even if the urgent application would occupy the computer system all the time, it makes sense to think about other needs early on, so that you can choose a system which is adaptable to other purposes. For the club, another headache is keeping track of the records of holidays which the club organises. In the present manual system, a record is kept of the name and address of each member booking, the state of their payments, and where they want to be picked up by the coach taking people to the airport. A sample record is shown below.

Records on each holiday are kept separately. So if a member is going on more than one holiday (which can happen, as they are spread over the year, with cheap rates for senior citizens), any changes may have to be recorded on more than one card. Bookings can be taken, not only at the club, but also by several of the organisers. As payments are made, these are banked in a separate account for each holiday – an account which never seems to balance correctly at the end. For each holiday, a list has to be made of pick-up points and the people to be collected there, which can itself be quite a tedious task when, as happened on the winter pensioners'

Seaside Sports and Social Club
Holiday Trips

Holiday: Bondi Beach   Mr A. B. Smith
Number in party: 3 adults   14 Berry Road
                  2 children   Parkway
                  2 senior citizens   SEASIDE
Date of departure: January 14 1984   PL13 2HH

Total cost of holiday: £3215.50
Deposit paid: £1100
Amount to pay: £2115.50

Pick-up point: Promenade

Figure 2 **Card used in manual system for holiday bookings**

special last year, over a hundred members went on the trip.

Other problems arose last year, because the people taking the bookings didn't always write them down correctly or remember to tell the holiday organiser, Donald, about them. Clearly this is one reason why the books don't always balance. It also means that holidays are over-booked very easily, or people missed off alto-gether. (On one occasion this was not discovered until Donald had an irate call from a would-be holiday-maker, who was still waiting at a rarely-used pick-up point half-an-hour after the coach had left the town.) Donald would like to prevent such muddles happening again. He would, however, still like to be able to take bookings at points away from the club, as this is more convenient for some members, especially the less mobile. Another problem can arise when people taking bookings away from the club don't pass the information over quickly enough. This can mean that Donald does not discover that a holiday is not proving very popular (and will therefore lose money if it goes ahead) until it is too late to cancel it.

Wherever bookings are taken, problems can also arise when a member moves house after booking the holiday and before taking it. This information may be given to the club secretary or typist, and probably entered on to the main membership record. But unless the member tells the holiday organiser as well, the holiday record is unlikely to get amended. It would be much easier all round if the change of address could be recorded once, and the correct address accessible to whatever processes needed it.

Gazing into the crystal ball

The two applications looked at so far are problems for which the club has devised a manual system, however primitive and ineffective. Another problem they would like help with is solved entirely 'by guess and by golly' at the moment, using no written records of any kind. The club has three bars in the main building, and runs two others at sports pavilions when matches are being played. Eventually they would like to have a proper stock control system, but before that they would like help with deciding how and where to buy their supplies. The difficulties arise because all the suppliers have a complicated system of special offers (especially at Christmas time). These could, if carefully exploited, make quite a difference to the profitability of the bars.

To make best use of the special offers, the club needs to collate information about suppliers and their products. For instance, a brand of whisky may be purchased from any one of half-a-dozen suppliers, each of whom also sells a wide range of other brands and types of spirits. Special offers often relate to the total value of an order, as well as to the prices of particular items. The club would like to find a quick solution to this immediate problem, and eventually to move to a complete stock control system.

In this chapter, we have looked at some applications which a small organisation – in this example a sports and social club – might have for a data management system. There were two reasons for doing this: to give you concrete examples of uses to which data management systems can be put, and to sketch the background to the specific examples used in the next part of the book. We have seen that the applications fall into three groups: an urgent requirement which needs top priority (the membership record system), a concrete but not quite so urgent need (the holiday bookings system), and a need which is strongly felt but which has not really been worked out at all (help in ordering bar stocks). All these problems will be used as examples in the detailed exploration of data management systems applications which follow.

Part 2
Information and its processing

In Part 1, we looked at an example of an organisation which felt it might benefit from introducing a computer to do simple information processing tasks. In Part 2, we look at the kinds of information which are commonly found in such applications of computers, and at the way computers handle the information. The aim is to help you see whether your information is suitable for computer processing, and what processing might be needed. In so doing, you should find out a lot about how computer packages actually handle information in practice, and thereby learn more about how to choose a package for yourself if this is appropriate.

It is unfortunate but inevitable that in this, and later parts, some technical terms must be used. Where these may be unfamiliar to you, they are shown in italic type, and an explanation is given in the glossary.

3 What sort of information? – A question of structure

*Your **starting point** in looking at a computer system for handling information is likely to be a **manual card index**. The **structure** of this card index may vary from the **completely regular** to the **completely unstructured**. Computer systems tend to demand a **more rigid structure** than is needed in manual systems, but repay these demands by allowing **more flexibility of processing**.*

Most people thinking about implementing a computer-based data management system already use some kind of manual system for their records. The most common is, of course, an index card. Whatever the physical medium, in order to keep the information compact and to be able to compare one card or record with another, the system is likely to involve some categorisation of the information. Thus each card in your card index box, or each form in your accounts file, is likely to have a similar appearance.

The cards may not be completely uniform, of course – some may contain a lot of information, others very little. For instance, if you are regularly despatching orders to customers, you may have a set of cards, each of which describes a customer. This may contain the customer's name, account address, delivery address if this is different, perhaps detailed despatch information if the customer has unusual arrangements – in manual systems, it is common to add little bits of extra information, such as 'don't deliver on Fridays'. These may not be an essential part of the system, but may help in its smooth running.

However, while a card index system can be pretty flexible about the type of information it contains, it is less easy to extract information from such a system except in its primary order, or to do calculations on numeric items on the card, or to add up such items across a set of cards. All these are, of course, functions which most data management systems carry out well. To gain these advantages, though, you will need to exploit the fact that information contained in records such as customer orders, sales accounts, stocks of goods for sale, personnel records, tends to have a fairly or completely regular structure. And in doing so, you will usually lose some of the flexibility of the traditional card index. In particular, you will usually have to be much more careful about the way in which information is categorised. For most systems expect you to predict what kinds of information you want to keep, and how much information each item will contain. Most systems also provide a limited number of categories for keeping your data, and these categories in turn constrain the ways in which the information can be manipulated.

To talk about such structured information in a coherent way, it is usual to employ three terms to describe the various aspects of the information and their storage on the computer. Each card or set of cards about a person, invoice, item of stock or whatever, is usually referred to as a *record*. Just as each card or group of cards in your card index has the same or roughly the same layout, each computer record will normally have the same or similar structure to all the others in one set of records. Such a set of records is usually stored on the computer in a computer *file* which corresponds to the box in which you would keep a manual card index. Within any one record, you will find items of information about each person, invoice, etc: each of these items will be stored on the computer in what is usually described as a *field*. An example of a card used in a manual card index is shown below; some items which would constitute individual fields are ringed. Each of these cards would be stored in a single record, and a set of such records would be stored in a single file.

So much for information with a regular structure. Card indexes are also used for information which is fundamentally less regular in its structure. For instance, a doctor may use such an index to take case histories; the card or cards might then contain just the patient's name and the date of consultation as identifying information, and otherwise consist of plain running text. Supposing the doctor is interested in finding out how many of his patients exhibit certain

```
Seaside Sports and Social Club

                                                    Mr A. B. Smith
Family member                                       14 Berry Road
                                                    Parkway
                                                    Seaside
                                                    PL13 2HH

Joined:  13 December 1983
Annual subscription:  £20.00
Years paid:  1983

Interests:  tennis, bowls, pool, table-tennis
```

Figure 3 **Manual record with regular structure**

symptoms (perhaps he is dealing with a local typhoid outbreak, and
wishes to identify all possible sufferers). Interview material of this
kind is often just reported 'straight from the horse's mouth', with no
categorisation at all. To extract the information needed, the
computer has to take an approach quite different from the processing of structured material, because both the material itself and the
user's processing requirements are likely to be very different.

The processing requirements are also likely to be less predictable
than in the case of structured information. The form in which the
information is needed after processing is usually very different too.
Where, say, an invoice is likely to need printing in fixed positions
across a page, with totals appearing below the columns of figures
they summarise, case histories and the like will need to be printed as
running text, with the input resembling that produced by a typewriter or word processor. An example of a manual index card with
such a format follows overleaf.

In between these two extremes of structured and unstructured
material lie a whole range of types of information which can conveniently be thought of as semi-structured, having aspects of both
structured and unstructured material. A library book catalogue, for
instance, often includes some fairly predictable information, such
as the author's name, the book title, date and place of publication

Mrs R. Jones   10 August 1983

Mrs Jones complains of backache and pains in the legs. These occur
especially when she is tired. P. has three children, no history of
prolapse. All children are at school. Husband is on night shifts.
Site of pain is usually lower back, extending occasionally into top of
leg. Changes of level when walking – stairs, etc. make it worse.
Relief possible by lying down. P. has full-time job, no rest
facilities at work. Examination showed site of pain tender, some
difficulty in bending. Referred for X-ray, make full gyn'l exam when
P. returns.

Figure 4 **Interview record card**

and so on. But it may also include a short summary of the subject of
the catalogue entry, as in the next example. Such records usually
require the processing functions applied to structured records for
the predictable information, plus the ability to treat items such as a
book abstract as running text. In practice, when data analysis is
needed, it is more likely that the information will have this mixture
of fixed items and running text rather than being completely unstructured. The choice of system will therefore depend on the
balance of processing needs.

Author: F. Brookes

Title: The Mythical Man-Month

Date of publication: 1976   Publisher: Addison-Wesley

Abstract: Most computer projects are not completed on schedule. Some
            reasons for this are examined, and some suggestions made for
            better methods in management and execution of large projects.
            Includes material on chief programmer teams. Based on
            experience of author in large project which he took
            over when already late.

Figure 5 **Library catalogue card**

In this chapter, we have looked at the different kinds of information which you may want to store in a computer system in terms of its regularity – structured, semi-structured and unstructured. Next, we shall look at how all three types of information can be stored and analysed using a data management system. The emphasis will be mainly on structured data, since almost all information needing computer processing is either structured or a mixture of structured and unstructured material. The special needs of analysing running text will not, however, be neglected.

4 Categories of information

*The implications of storing information on a computer depend on the structure of the information, and, within that structure, on what **categories** of information are involved. While reading about the types of storage and processing which are **possible**, you will also want to bear in mind the question of how to decide what should actually be stored **in practice**. The fundamental point to bear in mind here is your need for **extracting information and results from stored data**: it is pointless to store information which is not needed, either directly or indirectly, in your output from the system.*

The information most commonly found in structured material falls into four categories: numbers, characters, dates, and codes. Most data management systems expect you to state what sort of information each field is to contain, and permit different kinds of processing according to the type of data in question. Usually the first three types of information are stored because you need the information in its own right; the fourth kind, codes, is used to represent information indirectly, usually to economise on storage space, or as a way of identifying individual records so that it is easy for human users to cope with.

Numbers
Examples of numbers which you might keep in a structured record include a patient's height and weight in a medical record system, sums of money when processing accounts, and quantities of parts in stock in a garage stock control system. Numbers may be either whole numbers (integers) or have one or more figures after a decimal point (real numbers). Sums of money such as pounds-and-

pence, dollars-and-cents are usually expressed as real numbers with two figures after the decimal point.

Most data management systems expect you to be specific about the size of a numeric item – you must state how many digits the field will contain, and how many digits (if any) there will be after the decimal point. Some systems do not allow the use of a decimal point at all – all numbers are handled as integers. In these circumstances you have to treat real numbers as though they were integers, for instance by keeping all sums of money in pence, cents, or whatever is the smallest unit. Such systems are, not unnaturally, less convenient for handling information which contains real numbers. The other important aspect of the storage of numeric fields is the precision to which numbers are stored. Some systems allow only 7 or 8 digits, while others can store up to 14 or even 16. This point will need careful consideration, since in some systems this is an absolute limit on the number of digits which can be stored and displayed. If that is the case, it is not just a question of the accuracy of your figures, but rather whether they can be stored and processed at all.

Characters

Character information includes any form of words or letters. Character fields may usually contain any valid character which the system can represent, so they may well include numbers and special symbols as well as alphabetic characters. Examples of such fields include names, addresses, descriptions of parts, job titles and information describing the subject of an order or invoice. The number of characters which such a field may contain must usually be specified in advance. This is not always easy to do, as the person with the longest surname may not yet have joined your club. Unfortunately, most systems not only expect you to predict the maximum number of characters which each field will contain, but they also set aside this amount of space in each record you store, whether or not the space is actually needed. So the name Sym will take up as much space as Thompson-Cholmondeley-Smythe. This is much more of a problem when storing character fields, because although numeric items will also be stored in fixed length fields, they tend in practice to be much shorter. Not all packages do store information in this way – for instance, two widely available data management packages, *Pearl* and *CardBox*, both store only the actual characters needed for a field.

The other problem of which you should be aware is a **restriction** on the length of character fields. This varies from 32 to 1,024 among the packages which fix such limits, while others enforce no practical restriction at all.

However, you should not assume that the only criterion to consider is the amount of information which can be stored in a field. To process your information, the package must 'know' where each item in a record is located in the computer – otherwise it might print out a name when you wanted an address, or try to add up a set of job titles.

There are three basic ways in which this can be achieved: a diagram of the storage of our example club membership record in each of the three forms follows.

Smith01Mr		A.B.		Smith		
10	20	30	40	50	60

Fixed length record

Smith01,Mr,A.B.,Smith,14 Berry Road,Parkway,Seaside,PL132HH,

Variable length record

MN=Smith01 TI=Mr IN=A.B. SU=Smith AD=14 Berry Rd, Parkway, Seaside,

Tagged record

Figure 6 **Three approaches to storing items in computer records**

The first and most common of these approaches is to keep all fields in the same order within each record, and to use the same amount of space for any one item in each record. Such an approach is often referred to as using 'fixed length, fixed format records'. Then, when reading any individual record, the package knows which item is being processed just by counting characters from the beginning of the record.

The second approach is to have the items in each record stored in the same sequence, but to mark the end of each field value with a special character. This approach is said to use 'variable length, fixed format records', and allows the package to use only the amount of space the field requires. However, this means that the amount of space each record takes up is unpredictable. As records are deleted, new ones added, and existing records amended, the package must find appropriate free space for each record, without leaving 'holes' in the file and thus restricting the total number of records which can be stored. The accounting overheads of free space can be considerable: as a result, individual records may take longer to process, or you may periodically have to 'tidy up' the file by copying it.

The third possibility is to keep with each item of information some identifying characters which show what field value it represents. This approach, sometimes known as 'tagging', is used very effectively by the *SuperFile* package. However, it has disadvantages where the data may contain a very large number of different values, and is not common.

When considering methods of storing characters, you should also bear in mind the ways you need to process these fields. We shall look at this in detail in Chapter 7, but, for the moment, you should be aware that there are also problems in storing **too much** information in a single character field. This arises because some packages concentrate on providing ways of handling complete fields, and make little or no provision for handling parts of fields. So if you are storing, say, a customer's address, simply to print it out on an envelope or label when processing orders, you may have to keep that address in three or four separate fields corresponding to the lines you would want to print out. Similar considerations apply to retrieving records by complete fields or parts of fields.

These questions apply to the character fields themselves: in some circumstances you will need to consider what characters the system will allow you to store in those fields. Usually the system will be able to store all the characters in the basic *ASCII* set – though whether you will be able to see them all on the screen, activate them from your keyboard, and/or print them all on your printer will depend on the interaction of your computer with your data management system. If you are likely to want to store obscure characters – and on some systems 'obscure' may apply to such characters as the local currency symbol – you should check carefully that the system has that capability.

Dates and times

Most people need to store some date-based information: for instance the date of an invoice, of a consultation, of a course enrolment. Packages vary considerably in their ability to store and handle dates. Some have no special format for storing dates, while others just have one format, which may or may not be the format you normally use. This can be a particular problem for British users of American packages, as American software designers tend to assume that everyone uses their national convention in which the date is written as month/day/year, with two figures for each element. Thus 11th December 1983, which in Britain would normally be written 11/12/83, would appear in the American format as 12/11/83. Some packages avoid the problem by allowing users to specify one of several formats for the display of dates, including formats using letters – usually three – for the month, while storing dates internally in a code which is independent of the format used for display. *Delta* and *Everyman* are among the packages which have this flexibility.

Whatever its manner of display, it is usually helpful to have a special format for storing dates, as date arithmetic is then possible without too much effort. (You will appreciate that problems arise when treating dates as ordinary numbers, since effectively a date is three separate numbers, one to base 28, 29, 30 or 31 (depending on the number of days in the month), one to base twelve (for months in the year), and only the year is in the more usual base 10 in which we expect to do arithmetic.) Some systems, while not providing a special date storage format, do have facilities for processing numbers as dates, and this can provide a partial answer to the problem.

You will need to do arithmetic on dates where you want to calculate time spans, such as might be used in deciding whether a customer is entitled to prompt payment discount when paying a bill. It is also necessary if you are to store a person's date of birth and calculate age from that, in applications such as medical and personnel records. (It is much better to store date of birth rather than age if this is practicable, as date of birth does not change with time or need updating! This is one example of a general principle, that it is better to store fixed information and calculate varying information from it, rather than store information which varies in a predictable way.)

The other reason for wanting a special date format, if you need to store dates at all, is that with such a feature it is easier to order information by date (for instance to print a debtors' list ordered from the oldest invoices to the most recent). More about this in Chapter 7.

Most packages do have special arrangements for dates, but almost none have a special format for time. This is quite surprising, as of course minutes and hours are both recorded in units of 60 rather than 10, so ordinary arithmetic has the same drawbacks as it does for processing dates. If you need to process times – perhaps in a job costing application, or if your records are concerned with a professional practice such as that of a solicitor or architect – you will almost certainly have to choose a package which has a flexible approach to processing numbers. You will then be able to do arithmetic on time fields for yourself.

Codes

All the types of information looked at so far represent 'real' data values such as names, sums of money, dates of interviews, and so on. The last category to investigate consists of information which actually represents something else. There are usually two reasons for storing this kind of information.

In the first case, codes are simply representations at one remove of 'real' data. If you are processing a great deal of numeric information such as height, weight, etc., you may not be interested in the values to the nearest millimetre or gramme, but more in a range of values, say up to 5 kilos, over 5 kilos and up to 10, and so on. You

may then choose to store just the number 1 to represent a weight in
the first category, 2 for weights in the second category, and so on.
These codes are, of course, just numbers, and may be stored as
such. Equally, you may choose to store the information that a
person is male or female by using the single letters M or F, and this
time you can use a character field for that information. A more
complex example would be the registration plates of cars sold in the
UK between 1962 and 1983. All these plates contain a code of seven
characters, for example 'ABC473G'. The complete definition of the
permitted code range follows.

Character	Permitted value range
First	A-Z
Second	A-Z,space
Third	A-Z,space
Fourth	0-9
Fifth	0-9,space
Sixth	0-9,space
Seventh	A-H,J-N,P,R,S,T,V-Y

Definition of permitted range of codes on UK car registration plates

With this kind of information, the important thing is to be able to
check that the data entered into a field by a user does actually
conform to the specific format required. Packages vary tremendously in their ability to check the validity of information; if you are
faced with this kind of situation you should look at the more
detailed explanation of data validation in Chapter 15.

Codes are also used as a shorthand for identifying records. In a
manual card index system, you may use the name of a patient or a
member of staff or a customer, or of a car component for that
matter, as the heading on the card which you use to order the cards
in the box. It is, however, likely that you will have found using a
name to have drawbacks, for various reasons.

Ambiguity is one problem: lots of customers called Smith, or 6
different kinds of nearly identical washer. Consistency is another:
does Mr Johnson have a 't' in his name, or an 'e' on the end? This
kind of problem usually leads people, even in a manual system, to
choose some kind of code to identify individual records, such as an
account code consisting of the first three letters of the customer's

name together with a number starting from 1 to avoid ambiguity among all the Robinsons, Robbinses and Robsons. This approach is especially helpful in a computer-based system, where it is usually a little harder to browse through the records to find any that have been misplaced.

Systems vary substantially in their facilities for processing codes, whether we are talking about pre-processing raw data to turn it into coded values, or about codes used as a shorthand method of identifying particular records. The format of a coded value will be numeric or character depending on its range of values; a closer look at approaches to handling codes will be found in Chapter 6 (where we shall be looking at the use of codes for retrieving one or several records), and also in Chapter 15 (where we shall be considering ways to ensure that they are maintained correctly).

The illustration which follows overleaf shows a record for the club membership system, containing an example of each of the four types of field which can contain structured information.

Unstructured items

There are two main kinds of unstructured item you may wish to store. The first is essentially a list, such as the list of members' interests, where the list may contain no items or many, and where every element which is present is equally important and may appear in requests for retrieval. The second type consists of completely unstructured text, words within sentences, of indeterminate length. Some elements of such text are information-carrying words, which you are likely to need to retrieve, while other elements are connecting words such as 'the', 'and', 'but' and so on, which are usually of no significance in analysing the information.

It is possible to store unstructured text in character fields in ordinary fixed-length, fixed-format records. However, such an approach is usually appropriate only where the information is sufficiently predictable to make it possible to treat it as structured. Such information could be a list, such as our list of members' interests, or an item such as an address, where the information will need to be split into several fields for display, in this case on an envelope or label. Even where this approach is appropriate, many packages do not make it easy to process such fields, especially those

FORM LAYOUT (PAGE 1) FOR CLUBMRS

Club Membership Record System

Member's number_____1   Title_____2   Initials_____3

Surname_____4

Add1_____5   Add2_____6

Add3_____7   Postcode_____8

Date of joining_____9   Membership grade_____10

Date of last subscription payment____11   Amount of payment £____12

Interests_____13

Field	Name	Type	Width	Field	Name	Type	Width
1	Memnum	Code (Char)	7	2	Title	Character	10
3	Initials	Character	20	4	Surname	Character	30
5	Add1	Character	30	6	Add2	Character	30
7	Add3	Character	30	8	Postcode	Character	6
9	Datejoin	Date	7	10	Grade	Code (Char)	19
11	Datelastp	Date	3	12	Amtpayt	Numeric	7
13	Interests	Character	70				

Figure 7 **Club membership record containing four field types**

containing lists, in an appropriate way. Other packages have paid
particular attention to this area. A notable example is *CardBox*,
which allows you to store all your information in one field if you
wish, without artificial boundaries between bits of information
which are essentially contiguous. On the other hand, *CardBox* does
allow you to segregate information into fields if you wish, but you
pay no penalty for doing so – you don't, for instance, have to
remember in which field you entered the postcode before you can
search for it.

Such an approach can also be used for running text, provided the volume is small; *CardBox*, for instance, can store only 1,024 characters in a record. Sometimes the problem can be solved by splitting the information into several records, but this can create problems, both in duplicating identifying information and in associating all the records belonging to a single person, book or consultation. Where most or all of the information consists of running text, and the volume of each record is high, a different approach may be needed. Another package of particular value to those whose information is unstructured is *Search and Find*, a package which permits completely unstructured records to which the package builds up an index rather like the index to this book – only much more comprehensive, since it can if necessary include every word in every record.

However, using this kind of package has two distinct disadvantages. Firstly, it does not encourage you to use methods of compressing the information which will make it easier for you to analyse it later. Secondly, almost by definition such packages do not have any facilities for calculation. Thus, if you want to manipulate numbers as numbers (totalling them across records, for instance), you must consider adapting to a package which allows you some facilities for handling unstructured text while at the same time retaining the ability to store information in specifically numeric fields. We return to this subject in Chapter 8.

Information which has some inherent structure usually contains a mixture of numeric items, character items containing both letters and numbers, and dates; some of these items may actually be codes, which stand for a value rather than containing a value themselves. The importance of these distinctions lies in the ways in which you will be able to manipulate your information once it is stored. Generally, the more analytical you need to be, the more careful you must be to get the structure of your records right. This applies not only to the definition of individual items, but also to the structure of the record as a whole. Deciding how to divide your records into different groups is important too, and may have even more impact upon your ability to process your information. In the next chapter, we look at the storage of groups of items of information, and at the structure of groups of records.

5 Grouping items together

Items of information you wish to store in a record may be individual fields, or they may form part of a **group**. Two kinds of group are common: the **list** which may be one or more individual items grouped together under the same heading, and the **linked set of information**, which is connected with but separate from the main set.

In earlier chapters, we discussed sections of records in isolation, as fields of characters, codes, numbers or dates. We have assumed that each item of information is separate from the others, except perhaps in areas like addresses, where we looked briefly at the possibilities of using several fields, each for one printed line of an address. This kind of repeated field is actually quite common, and often occurs with information which requires a bit more processing than just displaying lines of an address.

Repetition most frequently arises in one of two ways. In situations like our club membership example, the need to repeat a field arose in storing information about members' special interests. With such fields (really lists), there are three problems to be tackled: the need to conserve storage space, the need to display only relevant information, and requirements for retrieval.

It is possible to store items in a list in several separate fields, allowing for the maximum number of items you are ever likely to need. (In our membership example, this would involve having perhaps six fields called Interest 1, Interest 2, etc.) Some packages, notably *Rescue*, have special facilities for checking this kind of information, and for ensuring that you do not see whole rows of blank fields displayed on the screen. Nevertheless, if fixed-length records are being used (as in *Rescue* and similar packages), this solution can take up large amounts of storage space. In most packages it is important to conserve space, as record size is commonly limited to 1,000 characters. This approach can also make processing difficult, because the package must allow you to select records on the basis that any one of your criteria is met – for instance, that Interest 1 contains 'pool' or that Interest 2 contains 'pool' and so on. Not all packages have this facility, as you will see in Chapter 7.

The alternative is to put the whole list in a single field. This will use no less storage space than putting the items in separate fields (that is, fixed length records may be very wasteful of space if these techniques are used). Storing the list in a single field does, however, mean that you need pose your question only once – does Interest contain 'pool'? This approach requires an easy method of searching for items within a field. In the last chapter we saw how one package achieves this, but many packages do not have this facility.

The two solutions looked at so far may be suitable when you have a list, containing several items relating to a record for one person, invoice or component. Repetition of information can also arise where a whole set of dissimilar items – perhaps including a list – recurs. The solutions described so far, methods of handling lists, are much less attractive where the amount of information occurring only once is small, and the amount of information recurring is much larger, as in a patient records system.

Here, you may have such items of information as name, address, sex, date of birth, known allergies and drug incompatibilities; these would be recorded only once for each patient. In addition, there may be information about each consultation the patient has with the doctor. Using one file for all the information, and conventional file formats whether fixed or varying, it would be almost impossible to allow enough space for each possible consultation. An alternative is to keep one record for each consultation, and store all the once-only items with information about each consultation. But this will give rise to two problems. First, the records will take up a lot of space, and the display of consultation records may be taken up with excessive information. Second, if any of the once-only information changes – if a patient moves, or a female patient marries and changes her name – each instance of that information will have to be found and changed, thus making it harder to be sure that each record is completely up to date.

In a manual system, it is most likely that this problem would be solved by having one card index for basic patient information, and another containing one card for each consultation, each kept in order of a patient identifier such as social security number. An example of a pair of such cards follows.

```
                                          Patient no. AABC24


Sex: Female                               Mrs R. B. Jones
Date of birth: 15 March 1951              12 Bay View Road
No. of children: 3                        Parkway
Year of most recent pregnancy: 1977       CHIMNEYTOWN
                                          BL10 6VB
                                          tel: Chimneytown 4356


Known allergies: house-dust
Drug counter-indications: penicillin
```

```
Mrs R. B. Jones        10 August 1983      Patient no. AABC24

Mrs Jones complains of backache and pains in the legs. These occur
especially when she is tired. P. has three children, no history of
prolapse. All children are at school. Husband is on night shifts.
Site of pain is usually lower back, extending occasionally into top of
leg. Changes of level when walking – stairs, etc., make it worse.
Relief possible by lying down. P. has full-time job, no rest
facilities at work. Examination showed site of pain tender, some difficulty in
bending. Referred for X-ray, make full gyn'l exam when
P. returns.
```

Figure 8 **Pair of records from manual card index**

In such a situation, one basic record is related to many subsidiary records, and is thus called a *one-to-many relationship*. A number of packages make explicit provision for storing such groups of information, protecting the user both from reserving large amounts of storage space which will not be needed, and from displaying information which is not currently relevant. Such packages are often said to carry out *transaction processing*, with each instance of repeated information (such as a consultation in the medical example) being regarded as a transaction attached to a single master record (such as the once-only patient information in the medical example). *Delta*, and *Tomorrow's Office* in its standard form, are examples of packages which store repeated information as transactions.

This problem of repeated records is not confined to one-to-many relationships such as one patient/many consultations. It is also found in situations such as a stock control and ordering system, where each item of stock may be bought from any one of several suppliers, and each supplier may supply several items of stock. The relationship between suppliers and products is then said to be a *many-to-many* relationship. If it were essential to cover this situation by keeping just one record for each stock item, you would have to assume some limit on the number of suppliers allowed per stock item, and store all the necessary supplier information for each supplier of a product in each product record. The amount of data duplication and hence wastage of space would, of course, be tremendous, with corresponding potential for error. Transaction processing systems are not usually sufficiently flexible to cope with this kind of relationship. Other packages are available for the purpose, handling the representation of relationships in various ways. *Everyman*, for example, enables the user to construct, for groups of records, a structure which is represented in diagrammatic form.

Approaches to storing and processing groups of records
There are three basic approaches to the handling of information with a complex structure. First, you can decide to use a simple package which does not allow you to link one set of records with another, and handle the linking problem in one of two ways. You can use the approach we discussed briefly above, of allowing enough fields in a single *flat file* (a file which models a single manual card index) to accommodate as many fields as you are ever likely to need. As we have seen, this approach uses a lot of storage space, and can be very limited in its processing capabilities. Or you can store each set of records in a separate file, thus mirroring the

approach you would have to use in a manual system. This would give rise to problems of keeping separate sets of information up to date, and of being unable to analyse the separate sets of records in harness. (For instance, in the medical situation, you might want to find out whether a particular disease occurs more often in women who have had children than in those who have not.)

The second basic approach involves using a separate file for each set of records, but relating information between or among files where appropriate. Again, there are several ways in which this can be achieved: all of them involve you in thinking about how to organise the relationships in detail, as well as in a bit of implementation work. To illustrate these approaches, we shall use the problem the club has with its holiday bookings system. The format used in the manual card index for holiday bookings is shown here.

```
                      Seaside Sports and Social Club
                              Holiday Trips

Holiday: Bondi Beach                              Mr A. B. Smith
Number in party: 3 adults                         14 Berry Road
                 2 children                       Parkway
                 2 senior citizens                SEASIDE
Date of departure: January 14 1984                PL13 2HH

Total cost of holiday: £3215.50
Deposit paid: £1100
Amount to pay: £2115.50

Pick-up point: Promenade
```

Figure 9 **Card used for holiday bookings**

Two contrasting approaches to handling linked sets of records using separate files are provided by the packages *Pearl* and *dBASEII*. *Pearl* handles the situation by allowing you to define a separate record format for each type of record, and then to specify that items in a record have to be 'imported' from other records. There are rules about how this can be done, to prevent circular definition or ambiguity about which records are related to one another. In the booking record shown above, some information – name and address – would normally be stored in the membership subscription record, and displayed but not stored with the holiday record. The two sets of records would be linked by membership number.

Other items in the holiday record, such as date of departure, would apply to every member on that holiday; these could usefully be kept in a separate file and recorded only once for each complete trip. They could then be displayed with each booking record, using the holiday code to find the correct information about departure date, etc. An example of a record format using this approach is shown below. The information above the first heavy line comes from the member record, that below the second heavy

FORM LAYOUT (PAGE 1) FOR HOLIDAY

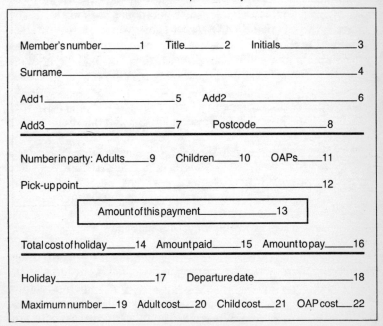

Club Membership Record System

Member's number_____1   Title_____2   Initials_____3

Surname_____4

Add1_____5   Add2_____6

Add3_____7   Postcode_____8

Number in party: Adults____9   Children____10   OAPs____11

Pick-up point_____12

Amount of this payment_____13

Total cost of holiday____14   Amount paid____15   Amount to pay____16

Holiday_____17   Departure date_____18

Maximum number____19   Adult cost____20   Child cost____21   OAP cost____22

Figure 10 **Booking record displayed with member and holiday information**

line comes from the holiday record, while that in the middle comes from the holiday booking record itself. (The numbers shown are simply the field numbers in this layout.)

However, the facilities for linking sets of records provided by *Pearl* permit you only to read from one file into another, not to write information into other records. There are circumstances in which this approach is inadequate. For instance, it would not be possible to total the payments recorded in each member's booking record, accumulate them for the whole holiday and store the aggregate total in the holiday record. You could get that information only through a report, which you would have to ask for each time you wanted it.

An alternative approach, taken by *dBASEII*, allows you both to read and to write to more than one file at a time, so that you could carry out such an operation. *dBASEII* uses commands to process files, which gives considerable flexibility at the expense of more work for you. In this example, some additional work might also be caused by the fact that *dBASEII* only allows you to process two files at a time. On the other hand, you don't necessarily want to display the member's name and address each time you make a booking entry. In the *Pearl* example, the display is set up that way because the package requires such an approach to permit access to information in several sets of records at once. So it is very much a matter of 'horses for courses', and we shall look at that question in more depth in Part 4.

Another approach to handling sets of records, where it is necessary to write as well as read more than one set from the same process, is provided by those packages which employ transaction processing methods. Using this approach, you create a master record to which many transactions can be attached. In *Delta*, one package which works in this way, you may have several different types of transaction attached to the one master record. However, information can only be passed between different types of transaction via the master record. So in our example you would have to choose between having the holiday record or the subscription record as the master, with the booking records as transactions. A format for a master/transaction record pair, with a master subscription record and a transaction record for booking and holiday information, is shown below.

DELTA file name: CLUBMHOL   File Title: Club members and holidays . . .
Date created: 12-12-83   Last updated: 12-12-83   Records used: 0
No. fields: 27   Rec. length: 427   Tran. groups: 1

Tran group	Field name	Fld type	Fld len	Tran group	Field name	Fld type	Fld len
1 0	Memnum................	C	7	2 0	Title.........................	C	10
3 0	Initials	C	20	4 0	Surname................	C	30
5 0	Add1	C	40	6 0	Add2	C	40
7 0	Add3	C	30	8 0	PC...........................	C	2
9 0	Datejoin	D	10	10 0	Mgrade	C	19
11 0	Datelastp	D	10	12 0	Amtpayt	2	6
13 0	Interests.................	C	70	14 1	Holname	C	20
15 1	Nadults	0	2	16 1	Nchildn...................	0	2
17 1	Noaps	0	2	18 1	Amtholpayt.............	2	6
19 1	Totcost...................	2	7	20 1	Totpaid...................	2	7
21 1	Topay.....................	2	7	22 1	Pickup....................	C	20
23 1	Depdate	D	10	24 1	Maxnum.................	0	3
25 1	Adcost....................	2	7	26 1	Childcst..................	2	7
27 1	OAPcost	2	7				

Figure 11 **Master/transaction record definition**

The third approach to repetition recognises the need to represent
complex relationships explicitly, and to have several levels of structure with communication from the lower levels up through the
higher. This approach is exemplified in the package *Everyman*,
which strongly discourages you from repeating information in different sets of records. The structure you need is set up in diagrammatic form: an example, a structure representing the club membership and holiday records, is shown below. The lower level boxes are
dependent on the levels above them, and can be reached only by
specifying the appropriate linking information. This provides, for
instance, an automatic check that someone booking a holiday is
actually a member of the club.

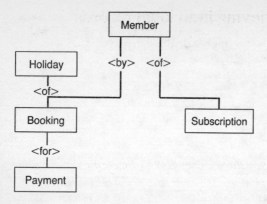

Figure 12 **Diagram of *Everyman* structure for club subscription and holiday records**

Each of these approaches to the storage of information with a complex structure has merits in particular situations. In this chapter, we have done the groundwork for assessing what kinds of structure could be most appropriate to your application. This will be built upon in Part 4. Meanwhile, we shall look at a number of aspects of processing information which apply to many kinds of structure, and at ways of processing information which has no structure at all.

6 Retrieving individual records

*The needs you have for **results** will dictate the ways in which you need to **retrieve** your information. In most applications, you will want to display and print individual records. The ways in which you want to do this will determine the most appropriate ways of storing records.*

The purpose of all data management is to put the results of data analysis and processing in the hands of those who need the information. So once you have thought about what kinds of information you need to handle, the next question is not, as most computer packages assume, exactly what to store and how to get that information into the computer, but what information you want to get out. The requirements for results – output, in computer terms – dictate the details of what you store and how it should be stored. In the next four chapters, therefore, we look at potential requirements, and at how reporting is handled by various types of data management package.

This chapter looks at the retrieval of individual records in applications where the information has an inherent structure. Subsequent chapters will look at retrieving and sequencing groups of records; at the special retrieval needs of unstructured records; and at requirements for layout and formatting of records when they have been retrieved. Finally, we shall look briefly at the problems of getting information out for subsequent re-processing, perhaps by another package on the same computer or on another computer.

What information do you want to get out?
A most important requirement is likely to be the need to look at individual records, either on screen or on paper. Information from a

traditional card index is either very simple or almost impossible. If you want to get information out in the same way, or in the same order in which it was indexed, you don't have a problem: you simply shuffle through the cards until you come to the correct entry. In this process, you do not search every record in order; you go to a point which you think will be close to your desired record, and then home in on the card you want. Of course, even when your card index is computerised you may still want to retrieve records in this indexed order, and most systems make that easy.

Finding individual records

If you are looking for an individual record, you will need some way of identifying that record. The quickest way to find a record in a computerised system is through a *key*, which just means one or more fields which have been nominated for the purpose. (The idea is, of course, that the key 'unlocks' the file for you and gives you entry into a particular record.) In our membership record system, the member's name was used as the key in the manual system, but names are not, as we have seen, ideal for this purpose.

Most packages on computers with floppy disk storage should be able to find an individual record through a key in under five seconds, and many take two seconds or less. On a hard disk system, retrieval time may be faster still. If the package has been well implemented, times for keyed access should be independent of the number of records you have.

The simplest form of key is a reference number, allocated by the system when the record is first entered. This gives you both the ability to look through the records in entry order, and the ability to find a particular card by giving its reference number. In the simplest models, this number starts at one and is increased by one each time a record is added. In practice this is an unsatisfactory way of finding individual records, still less groups of records, for several reasons.

First, to see or print an individual record, you have to remember – or have readily available on paper – the number of a record you want to get at. Second, since numbers are less *mnemonic* – memorable in relation to what they stand for – than codes or letters, they are also more likely to be entered incorrectly. Third, when you want to look at several records, order of entry is unlikely to be the order you need. (It rarely is the process you go through with a manual system, where you are more likely to have cards in, say, member name order and to need the card for a particular member.) Fourth, what happens about deleted records? In some systems, the number of a record you have removed is left unused, so that records retain their original reference number. On most systems, however, the number is re-used to make it easier for the package to carry out processing requirements which apply to every record.

There are circumstances in which it is useful to be able to scan through your records in entry order, for instance in checking invoices. However, it is unlikely to be easy to find individual records in this way, nor is it convenient to have to specify an arbitrary number. An alternative is to decide that one particular field will be the main way of finding any one record. This field may contain the name of the author of a book, the NHS or social security number of a patient, or the name of a club member. This is, of course, the way a manual card index works. You decide how the cards are to be kept in the card index box, and this enables you to find a particular book, patient or member by checking through this identifying field. In those data management packages which use a single field as the main way of identifying individual records, this field is called the *primary key*.

The criteria for deciding which field shall be the primary key are very similar to those in a manual system. The objective is to select an attribute which will identify the record uniquely, relate closely to the 'real world' information, and be easy to enter into the computer without making mistakes. Some applications have an element which is a natural candidate for being the primary key: medical records, for instance, would in the UK record the National Health Service number of the patient, while in other countries it is common practice to use the social security number. Another example would be a part number used when ordering a motor car component from the supplier. The manual index card which follows shows an example of a component record, with the part number ringed. This identifying 'number' may actually be a code consisting of numbers and letters. Its principal attributes should be that it is an item which will be stored with the patient's history or part description anyway, and is unique to that patient or component. Another

```
┌─────────────────────────────────────────────────────────┐
│                 Barney's Expert Garage Repairs           │
│                       Component Record                    │
│                                                           │
│                              Part number: 74AB435W/81     │
│                              Location: Bay 3 Shelf 9      │
│                                                           │
│   Current quantity: 30 29 28 27 26 25                    │
│   Re-order level: 20                                      │
│                                                           │
│   Description: Left-hand washer for knurl-knut           │
│                                                           │
│   Supplier: A. B. Barnett                                 │
│             Foundry Works                                 │
│             Brunel Trading Estate                         │
│             SOLIHULL                                      │
│                                                           │
└─────────────────────────────────────────────────────────┘
```

Figure 13 **Component record with unique part number ringed**

advantage is that this kind of code is likely to be used by others
supplying information about the subject. In the example of patient
care, an instance would be a hospital where the patient has been
referred for specialist treatment. The hospital is certain to have its
own manual or automated records system, and it may be that the
only item the records have in common is the patient's code number
and name.

For records about people, the person's name is another obvious
candidate for use as the main method of retrieving individual
records. However, names are not ideal for this purpose, since it is
hard to render names unique without making them difficult to enter
and remember. For instance, if you have many people called Smith,
you may decide to include their initials in the name. So you enter a
name as AMSmith. When you subsequently ask the package to
find AMSmith, it can't. Why? Well, if you look carefully, you will
see that in the first reference to Smith there are spaces after each
initial and its associated full stop, while in the second there are no
spaces.

While it is obvious to human eyes that the two names are the
same, the package cannot tell. Its method of testing is a character-
by-character comparison between name as entered and name as

stored; this test for identity will fail when the package tests the third character in each of the two values of 'name'. The same problem would, of course, arise if you typed A M Smith – or, for that matter, a. m. smith. (However, many packages let you choose to 'ignore case', that is to treat upper and lower case letters as identical for the purpose of finding a particular key item. Others always ignore case in this situation, which can lead to incorrect matches.)

Serious problems of ambiguity can also arise – most people no longer spell their own names in as many different ways as Shakespeare reputedly did, but that does not avoid all misspellings. So you may retrieve a unique record in response to a request for information about a particular person, but is it the right person, record or relationship between them? Another difficulty is that using as a key an item such as name-and-initials, which is actually two items, may give rise to problems when designing printed reports. For instance, suppose you want to include some information from your records in a 'personalised' letter – perhaps to remind members that their subscriptions are due. Since few packages allow you to display or print part of a field, you would be forced either to write to 'Dear A.M.Smith', or to record the name twice, once as 'name-and-initials' to be used as the primary key, and again as 'title-and-name' so that you can write to 'Dear Mrs Smith'.

Packages use various methods of circumventing these problems: *SuperFile*, for instance, allows you to make a search for a field value which 'sounds like' the value you are looking for. So a request to find Johnston would also find Johnstone, thus freeing you both from the problems of spelling and from the need to use a composite field as the key. However, this facility may conflict seriously with the need to have a unique primary key, and indeed those systems which allow such methods of retrieval generally avoid the uniqueness problem by not requiring the key field to be unique. You are then left with the need to look through several records to find the particular one you need – like looking through all the cards for authors whose name is Jones.

The lesson of all this is that if your information includes an item which would naturally form a unique primary key (such as social security number, component identifier, membership number), it may be appropriate to choose a package which uses such a key to find individual records. If your information does not include such a field, you may want to use a different approach. One possibility is to devise a code which is a combination of easily remembered characters with some device for ensuring that any one record has a unique code. For instance, you might use the first five characters of each person's name, followed by two digits allocated in ascending order as each person's details are recorded. This would give a code of Smith01 for the first person called Smith who was entered in your records, Smith02 for the second Smith, and so on, while people called Johnson would go in as Johns01, Johns02, etc. A record for the membership subscription system would, if this approach were used, look like the example which follows. The first field, Member's Number, contains the seven-character code.

FORM LAYOUT (PAGE 1) FOR CLUBMRS

Club Membership Record System

Member's number____1 Title____2 Initials____3

Surname____4

Add1____5 Add2____6

Add3____7 Postcode____8

Date of joining____9 Membership grade____10

Date of last subscription payment____11 Amount of payment £____12

Interests____13

Figure 14 **Membership record using member code**

Another possibility is to use a package which permits duplicate key field values. Your key can then be an item which is inherently ambiguous, such as a name. The corresponding disadvantage is that, when looking for a particular name, you may be presented with several options from which to choose.

The extent to which you may have problems with ambiguity will also depend on the action taken if no exact match is found for the key value entered. Some systems give an error message, others assume that you wish to create a new record with that key value. The most helpful approach is to give you the 'nearest' value. This usually means that if, say, you ask to find someone called Robins, and there is no Robins but there is a Robinson, you will get the Robinson record. If the package then allows you to request the 'next forward' or 'next backward' record, you can explore, and by displaying just a few records find the record you were really seeking. However, if your failure to find the desired record occurs because it has been incorrectly entered, browsing through in primary key order may not help. For instance, if you typed Dimon instead of Simon, the record would be stored in completely the wrong place.

An alternative approach, used by more sophisticated packages, allows you to use several fields in conjunction as a key. In our example of using names, you would have separate fields for surname and initials, but use the two together as the key. This does not, of course, help with the problems of misspelling. It does, however, make duplicate names less likely, without the need to lump together fields which must afterwards be printed or processed separately.

So far, we've been looking at the retrieval of individual records in ways which you should be able to predict when the computer system is first set up. However, you may also want to find individual records in other ways. For instance, a member pays his subscription without telling you his membership number. So all you have is his name, in a system where the primary key is the membership number. In a manual card index, kept in order of membership number, you would have to look at each card to find which member had paid you. In a computer system, you could use the same approach. But it will save you much time if the computer can, without your intervention, check each record in turn to find the required name.

This process, usually termed *sequential access*, is much faster than its manual equivalent, but still slower than using a key to go directly to the required record. Factors affecting the speed of sequential access include the efficiency of the package itself, the number of records you have stored, the speed with which your computer can read information stored on its disks, and the amount of comparison which has to be done. (For instance, if you are looking for someone called Brown, there may be several other members with the same name, and the system will then have to compare initials as well.) Speed of retrieval using this approach varies far more between packages than does retrieval by key – more about this when we look at selecting groups of records in Chapter 7.

In many systems, this method of checking each record in turn is the only way to select an individual record other than through the primary key. However, more powerful packages allow you to specify several different fields (or groups of fields) as keys, so that you can quickly retrieve any record using several alternative approaches. In our membership example, we might decide to use as a key both the membership number and the member's name. Then we could display the record quickly whether the member included his or her membership number, or whether we had to search just on name.

This very useful facility has one potential drawback. To allow access to individual records directly by one or more keys, the usual approach is to create an index to the file for each key. One way to construct such an index is to have a small separate file which consists of a list with two entries for each record, one entry being a reference number (like the page number in a book index) and the other the value of the key field for that record. The entries in the index file are stored in order of the value of the key field. The diagram which follows shows how the primary order of records and of an index relate to one another.

Whenever a new record is entered, the system must also add an entry to the index file, consisting of the new record's reference number and key field value. When a record is deleted, a corresponding pair of deletions must take place. However, some systems which allow this facility are able to keep up to date only the index for the primary key field, not any other indexes on other fields. These subsidiary indexes must be re-created after any records have been added or deleted, or if changes are made to the values of indexed fields. There are several disadvantages to this approach: recreating an index takes time (sometimes quite a long time), you have to

Record no.	Key field value
1	Dogwo01
2	Zebra01
3	Antel01
4	Smith01
5	Beave01
6	Albat01

Record no.	Record no. in data file	Key field value
1	6	Albat01
2	3	Antel01
3	5	Beave01
4	1	Dogwo01
5	4	Smith01
6	2	Zebra01

Part of records
in data file

Records in index file

Figure 15 **Diagram of relationship between data and index files**

remember to do it (though some packages are able to tell you that an index has become out of date) and the need to do so becomes yet one more procedure for the novice user to learn. Even those packages which can keep several indexes up to date may have to be told explicitly that you wish to do so, something which may get forgotten.

So why does every package not provide the ability to access records directly through any field, and keep the indexes up to date automatically? The answer is that you pay a price for speed of access and flexibility. The price is in extra time when a record is added or changed, and in extra storage space for the indexes. Whether these factors are significant will vary a good deal between one package and another. The worst aspect of the problem is that the more additions and changes are being made, the more important it is to keep indexes up to date, otherwise you will constantly be re-creating them. Yet, if you are making a lot of changes, you will lose more time overall in that 'housekeeping' than if your data were relatively stable.

Two lessons can be learnt from this discussion. First, it matters much more that retrieval of records should be fast when you are using the package directly, that is, when you are sitting at the computer looking at information on the screen, than when you are printing reports which you can leave to 'get on with it' by them-selves. So if you only need to look at records on the screen using one field for direct access, then it usually doesn't matter so much if the package allows fast access by only one field. Even when a package is reading each record in turn to pick out those which you want to print out, it is unlikely to take a long time to find a record in relation to the time it takes to print it out. (This may not hold good if your file is very large – when reading sequentially, most packages are slow to find one record among tens of thousands.)

Second, if you really do need fast access on the screen to records through several fields, choose a package which permits you to have several key fields and which keeps them up to date automatically. But make sure that before you buy it you see the package working on a reasonably large quantity of information, with several indexed fields, so that you can check that the time taken to store a new or changed record is acceptable. You should also check the amount of space needed for the indexes: they may use up a sizeable amount of disk space which would otherwise be available for your records.

In this chapter we have looked at various ways of retrieving individual records in situations where the information has a regular structure. The options include allowing the system to allocate a unique reference number, using a single primary key which must have a unique value, or relying on combinations of several fields to avoid ambiguity while providing flexibility. Such features may give limited access to groups of records by allowing you to look through records in key order. More extensive facilities for retrieving groups of records are discussed in the next chapter.

In addition to finding individual records, you will want to retrieve **groups of records** *which conform to a given specification. You may also need to display or print records in a particular* **sequence**, *which may not be the order in which they are stored. Another requirement may be for* **summarising** *records by totalling or averaging numeric fields, or counting the occurrence of values. In addition, you may want only to retrieve a* **part of each record**.

Finding groups of records

Using a key to find a record, and then browsing through the records before and after the record you have accessed directly, is one way of finding a group of records. A more deliberate approach is to set up a specification for a set of records in a formal way. For example, you could ask for 'the records of all members who are more than three months overdue with their subscriptions' or 'all the members who are available to play in the table-tennis team next weekend' or 'all the club members who are eligible for life membership, because their total subscriptions have reached the agreed level'. Packages vary quite a bit in how formal this request must be. There are three main approaches, with some minor variations on those themes.

The most formal and cumbersome approach involves setting up a request which is then saved in a special *selection criteria* file. When the request is carried out, the set of records which meet the criteria are written to a new data file, which you may subsequently display or print. This can take some time. The second approach also involves setting up a request which is saved. You may then ask for the request to be processed, whereupon the selected records are displayed or printed according to your instructions, though no new approach, but to permit the selection of a particular save for subsequent re-use, in cases where this is a regular task.

There is also considerable variation in the kinds of request that the user can make. The basic form of a request will involve testing each record to see if it meets one or more criteria for selection. A test will consist of the name of a field, an operator, and the value against which the field is to be tested. For number and date fields, operators are typically the 'comparison operators' – less than (<), greater than (>), equals (=) and combinations of these, together with 'not equals'. The value against which the field is to be tested may be a number or date included in the selection request, or it may be the value of another field in the record, or the value of some other item such as 'today's date'. An example might be a request to find all those whose holiday payments are less than the total cost of the holiday, with the test looking like this:

Show all records where Total-paid < Total-cost

In systems which can do date arithmetic correctly, you can, for example, ask to see 'the records of all members whose subscriptions are overdue' by getting the system to test for 'subscription-date < today's-date'. You would then be presented with the record of each member whose subscription date preceded the date today.

Some or all of these operators may be available when testing fields containing characters; all packages permit you to test that two character fields are identical. However, equality between character items does not necessarily mean the same as equality between two numbers. As we saw when looking at retrieving records by key, such tests are affected by whether or not we care about differences in punctuation and spacing, and about exact matching of the characters themselves. Many packages allow you to ignore case when comparing characters, that is to treat upper- and lower-case letters as equivalent. Some packages, on the other hand, assume this between exact matching and approximate matching, and the ability to include 'wild codes'. The distinction between exact and approximate matching varies among packages. A common approach to a request for approximate matching is to retrieve those records which match exactly, and also those where the field **contains** the set of characters being matched. (For example, a request for all members interested in 'tennis' would, if an exact match were used, simply find all members interested in tennis. If an approximate match were requested, however, the system would also locate all members whose interests included 'table-tennis'.) In other packages, an approximate match would find just those records where the field **started with** the characters in question. (A request for people interested in 'singing' would in that case find those interested in 'singing folk songs' and in 'singing madrigals', but not those interested in 'part-singing'.)

The most comprehensive form of selection of character fields involves 'wild codes' (sometimes called 'wild cards', in an allusion to the practice of allowing the jokers to stand for any card in some card games). Using this method, you may enter a symbol which can stand for any character or group of characters. A field which matches the test item in other respects will then be regarded as meeting the criterion. (For example, to find all the members who were interested in any form of skating, you could test for interest being equal to ★skating, where ★ is a wild code. You would then see the records of all members interested in roller-skating, ice-skating, etc., as well as just plain skating.)

The ★ symbol is very commonly used for this purpose; another common symbol is the question-mark, which is allowed to stand for just one character rather than 'none, one or more characters'. (The use of these symbols is a sensible extension of the practice generally used in microcomputer operating systems when looking for groups of files during a directory command.) However, if you need to be specific about the positioning of information in a long field, it is tedious to have to enter a question-mark for each character whose

Searching for: pool

Method 1: search for 'string starting with' would not find pool
Method 2: search for 'string within' would find pool, because 'pool' is contained within the field
Method 3: search for *pool* would find pool as in Method 2

If you remember that a member's **Surname** begins with 'S' and ends with 'son', but can't remember if it is Smithson, Simpson or Stimpson:

Method 1: Can only find all surnames starting with 'S'
Method 2: Can either find surnames beginning with 'S', or those ending with 'son', unless package allows you to apply more than one test to the same field
Method 3: Searching for 'S*son' will find all the possible records

Figure 16 **Examples of matching parts of fields**

Sometimes, you will want to make more than one comparison on a record before it is allowed to pass or fail the test. When this is so, there must be some way to determine how tests are to be combined. Supposing you want to find all the members who play table-tennis **and** are normally free on Friday evenings. This would involve selecting only the records which pass both tests. In the sentence describing the test I used the word 'and'; this is actually the term often used in a package to say that both conditions must be met. However, an alternative possibility would arise if you wished to find the records of members who were interested in table-tennis **or** pool, so that records would be selected if they passed either test. Again, the word 'or', used in the description of the test, is often used to express this connection. Some packages allow only the 'and' connector, so you can select only those records which pass all tests. You should therefore give some thought to your likely needs for combining tests. Some examples of tests using more than one criterion follow.

'pool'$Interests .and. (Title='Mrs' .or. Title='Miss')

'swimming'$Interests .and. Title<>'Mr'

(!(Mgrade)='FAMILY' .or. !(Mgrade)='INDIVIDUAL') .and. .not. 'pool'$Interests

Figure 17 **Tests involving several criteria**

Selecting information from related files

Where information fits comfortably into *flat format* files, without repetition of fields, this problem can be ignored. If, however, your data is structured in one of the ways we looked at under Groups of Items in Chapter 5, you will need special methods for describing records which are dependent upon 'master' or 'superior' records. The most common way of doing this is to retrieve the information via a hierarchy of data units: transaction records will be retrieved with the master record to which they relate, dependent records with reference to the values of their superiors. This approach will be described more fully in Part 4, when we look at a real application based on these approaches.

Sequencing the information

When you display or print selected groups of records or the whole set, you may want to see the records in a particular order. For instance, when selecting those members whose subscriptions are overdue, you may wish to see those selected in order by date, with those most overdue appearing first. Or you may wish to see a list of those interested in a particular activity appear in alphabetical order of the member's name. Unless you give alternative instructions, records are likely to appear ordered by the primary key, or, if there is no primary key, by the order in which the records were entered. Two approaches to showing records in a new order are common. The obvious option is to sort the records into the new order. This would be the only possible technique with a manual card index, where you would simply shuffle the cards into a new order based on the *sort criterion* you required.

Such shuffling is not an ideal approach in any situation, though, as it involves physically moving each record, often several times, and this can take a long time even on a computer system. (I have used packages which have taken several hours to sort a file of 1,000 records in order on one field, though that is exceptionally slow – the typical time is about 20 minutes.) In addition, you will need to go through the sort process all over again each time you add extra records to the data file.

An alternative is to extract from the main file the record number of each record and the value of the field to be used for sorting, and then sort those small records into a separate file. This process is usually much faster (of the order of a few minutes for a file of the size mentioned above). It is also, as observant readers will realise, very similar to that used to create an index to allow direct access to records on a particular key field or fields. A number of systems therefore use the same approach to both. So when accessing a file using a particular index you gain fast access to individual records, and in addition records appear to be sorted in order by the current key field. As a result, the comments in the previous chapter about keeping indexes up to date apply also to indexes created for the purpose of retrieving groups of records in a particular order.

Summary information
So far, we have been thinking about showing the values contained in records just as they were entered. Often, you will also want to produce summary information. You may want to **count** the number of records in a particular category, or **total** a field such as the subscriptions paid. Some packages allow you to get out this kind of information only in company with some information about each record – they assume that you will only need summary information as part of a printed report, which includes information about every record to be summarised. It can be very useful to be able to get summary information alone, especially as this may then be obtainable much more quickly than getting details about every record.

For example, supposing you wanted to count the number of members whose grade is 'Family'. Using a command provided in both *dBASEII* and *Condor*, you could say:

Count for Mgrade = 'Family'

and the package would respond by displaying the number of members in that category. *Condor* has an extended version of that facility, which allows you to tabulate the records by the values of

one or two fields. The example below shows a summary of numbers
of members in each grade.

Tabulate members by grade

Mgrade

		(Count)
Individual		92
Family		237
Senior citizens		130
Playing		73
	Total	432

Figure 18 **Summary of members in each membership grade**

You may also want to carry out simple calculations interactively: for
example, you could find the average amount of subscription paid by
each member who has made a payment at all. The next example
shows how you might carry out such a calculation.

```
.count for amptpayt>0 to paidmems
COUNT=213
.sum amtpayt to totpaid
  2563
? totpaid/paidmems
  12.0328
```

Figure 19 **A calculation carried out on demand**

Some packages which do not allow you to carry out this kind of
calculation interactively do give you such facilities when producing
formatted reports, and almost all packages are then able to calculate totals and sub-totals. More will be said about this in
Chapter 10.

Selecting parts of records
In addition to selecting groups of records, you may also want to
select particular groups of fields for display. For instance, if you
were selecting the records of members whose subscriptions were
overdue, you would probably need to retrieve only their names,

addresses and the sums of money owing. You could then use this information to send reminder notes. Some packages allow you to do this interactively, as in the example below, which shows a command to display the names of those lady members who play pool, together with the resulting list of names.

.Display for 'pool'$Interests .and. (Title='Mrs' .or. Title='Miss') Surname

Albatross
Dragon
Eagle
Fox

Figure 20 **Displaying selected fields from selected records**

However, many packages allow you to be selective about which fields you see only as part of a reporting mechanism which is intended for producing printed output. Since printing is essentially a 'batch' process, carried out without intervention from the user, these reports are usually created by first setting up a format and then issuing the report. You can usually display these reports on the screen first, but such display is still a two-stage process. This can be rather inflexible if all you want is a simple list on the screen of, say, the names and arrears of your current debtors so that you can telephone those who have owed the most for longest.

Even more inflexible are those packages which allow you to be selective about which fields you display on the screen only if you create a separate file consisting of those records and fields which you wish to display. This can be quite a lengthy process (15–30 minutes), so if you will often want to select fields for screen display then you should think carefully before choosing such a package.

In this chapter we have looked in some detail at the needs you might have for retrieving individual records and groups of records, and for inspecting those records in varying sequences. Most of this material applies only to information with a clear structure, and not to less structured material such as text summaries. However, such material does need to be retrieved selectively, and we shall look at those needs in detail in the next chapter.

8 Retrieving unstructured information

*The requirements for retrieving unstructured information are quite different from those encountered when analysing structured records. Typically, unstructured text tends to involve **large amounts of information**, and the major problem is to find ways of providing **fast access to key words**.*

In the last two chapters we looked in depth at the problems of retrieving information which has an inherent structure. We shall next look at the question of retrieving and analysing information with no inherent structure beyond that normally found in written text – words, phrases, sentences, paragraphs.

Structured information is normally analysed in terms of items or fields of data within records, each of which is identical in form with or very similar to every other record which needs to be processed. Text does not have this kind of format at all. Among the circumstances in which you might want to analyse text, the most common involves catalogues such as those found in libraries. Here the requirement might be to scan a whole series of abstracts to discover sources of information about a particular topic. Other situations in which this need arises include directories of many kinds such as restaurant guides, gazetteers, lists of people in particular professions, product descriptions, transcriptions or summaries of patients' case histories or of personnel interviews, records of committee meetings. Such material tends to contain large amounts of information, and to have little or no structure beyond division into individual words (though it may be associated with structured material, such as the name of a book, restaurant, firm, or product).

It also contains a proportion of words which are not of interest, such as 'and', 'the' and so on.

In these circumstances, the need is to select records which conform to certain specifications. (In this respect, the problem is similar to that of selecting groups of structured records.) For example, if you have stored a set of minutes of committee meetings, you might want to find all references to a particular point under discussion. In our social club example, we might want to locate all the occasions when the committee discussed changing subscription rates.

In Chapter 4 we saw that, in some circumstances, it is possible to treat elements of unstructured information in a similar way to structured data. Using an approach comparable to that used in structured records, you could decide which key words were of particular importance in the text, and store those in separate fields, each of which could be checked individually. However, that puts a premium on deciding in advance which words or topics are going to be significant. Such predictability is very hard to achieve with text. On the other hand, it is not practicable to store in an individual field each word in a section of running text (such as an abstract). Nor is it appropriate, since the text may contain phrases which need to be considered either as a whole or as consisting of their component words. Usually, therefore, the whole of the abstract is stored as a single entity. The need is then to be able to search for individual words or phrases within that entity.

It is possible to find such words or phrases by searching each record sequentially, noting matches as the search progresses. However, the sheer volume of information makes this a very slow process. For instance, an abstract typically contains about 200 words, each of which may be significant in the search process. Where many abstracts are involved, a sequential search can take a very long time. The problem is to find rapid methods of search (usually via indexes), which do not at the same time constrain the user too much, or make it unlikely that the desired reference will be found. Several packages make special provision for such situations, each differing considerably in their approach. Here we shall look at two which provide an interesting contrast, and use their approaches to highlight various aspects of the problem of extracting information from textual material.

The approach taken by the *CardBox* package is to regard the text as one element in a potentially structured record. A record may if necessary consist of only one field. A *CardBox* field may thus be much larger than those permitted in most conventional data management packages – up to 1,024 characters in all. The whole of a field, or any word within a field, may be indexed and hence used to retrieve the record directly. The user is given considerable control over which words will be referenced directly, that is over which words will be stored in the index. It is also possible to index complete phrases.

Once information has been entered and indexed, it can be searched in a variety of ways. You can search for a particular reference in a single field; if any match is found, the package will tell you how many references have been found and display the first matching record in the file. Sometimes such a search will not have been phrased sufficiently exactly, and will result in the package finding perhaps several hundred records which match. You can then specify another set of conditions, which will be applied only to those records which matched the first test.

On the other hand, you may have set the criteria too narrowly, and found only one or two records which match; if you are looking for a reading list on a particular subject, or a range of restaurants to recommend to your friends, you may then want to extend the search a little, without actually starting again. *CardBox* allows you to request a further selection from the records which were not chosen on the first round of tests.

The material may also have been divided fairly arbitrarily into fields. Even with names and addresses, it is not always possible to ensure that the post town always appears on a particular line of the address fields, to allow you to search for 'all those who live in Manchester'. In *CardBox* the indexing methods allow you to search for information within a specified field, or anywhere in the record.

However, you pay a price for this flexibility: as each record is entered, decisions must be made about what to index. This contrasts with the process of entering structured records, where this decision is made once, and operates for every record in the file. You may therefore spend more time on data entry in *CardBox* than might be strictly necessary, depending on the nature of your information. In addition, the allowance to 1,024 characters for each record might be insufficient.

An alternative approach is used by *Search and Find*, which is intended for applications where the material to be analysed has no structure at all, that is plain running text only. Here the approach is to separate the entry of information from the indexing process. Text is entered separately using a word processor, then indexed by *Search and Find* in a batch process without intervention by the user. The units involved in the indexing are word within document. Files are not divided up into records and thence into one or more fields as in *CardBox*; each document is stored in a separate file, with a title which is used to identify the document during retrieval. (This means that the restriction on the size of a unit of text – a document – is only that imposed by the computer system on file size. However, on floppy disk systems this technique may restrict the number of documents you can search at any one time, since you will usually be restricted to a maximum of 128 documents on one floppy disk.) In order to avoid wasting time indexing words which will never be used to retrieve information, you can set up a 'stop list' of words which should not be indexed, such as 'and', 'the', 'not', etc.

Retrieving information in *Search and Find* is a two-stage process. Firstly, you specify the search you want to make; the package then tells you how many documents conform to that specification. You can then restrict the search criteria further if you wish, or widen it; in the latter case, you will also be told how many documents meet both your criteria. If you wish, you can then see the titles of all those documents which contain the references you require. So in the example of the need to search committee records, you would get a list of all those meetings at which the subject was discussed. To view the documents themselves, you use the direct link between *Search and Find* and your word processor, and inspect or print them using that program. This means, of course, that should you wish to amend your search criteria after inspecting the documents retrieved, you must then return to *Search and Find* for more searching. (The advantage is that word processing functions are not replicated within the package, thus avoiding the need for additional learning.)

These approaches are, of course, sufficiently different to be appropriate to quite contrasting situations. The *CardBox* approach is best suited to records with a fairly small amount of running text, mixed in with structured material, where you want to be able to see your retrieved records during the search, and where you need direct control over the indexing process. Examples would include most kinds of directory and gazetteer entries, book catalogues, and case histories and personnel interview records which contained abstracts rather than verbatim records of interviews.

The *Search and Find* method is, by contrast, more suited to longer documents which have little or no inherent structure, such as minutes of meetings, literature references containing extended descriptions, and interview records based on transcriptions or extended summaries. In such situations you are more likely to be able to allow the package to take care of indexing without intervention, and be content to switch between the package and a word processor in order to view information you have retrieved.

In this chapter we have been concerned with the considerations involved in retrieving and analysing unstructured material. We look next at the ways in which material can be displayed once it has been retrieved. This topic is covered in the next two chapters.

9 Displaying information

A central theme of this book is the importance of being able to get out the results you want. In this chapter, we shall look at the ways in which you may display information on the screen, and print simple copies of screen displays.

In most applications of data management, the needs for display and printing are fourfold. You will need to display individual records for inspection or processing on the screen, and to look at lists or summary information for quick checking, also on the screen. You will also need to print individual records and lists, using more sophisticated layout to make the output more presentable to others. (Perhaps the information may be needed by other people who will use it over a period of time, or by people outside your organisation.) In this chapter we shall look at the question of screen display, while in the next two chapters we shall discuss requirements for printing. We shall also refer to the ways in which selection requirements (discussed in Chapter 7) are implemented in practice, for screen display and for printing, since not all packages allow the same facilities in both. The emphasis throughout will be on the features themselves; in Chapter 16 we shall look at how such facilities may be set up.

Displaying records on the screen
Clearly you will need at least one layout or format for showing records on the screen; this simply corresponds, in your manual system, to the layout of the information on the index card. It can be very helpful to design alternative formats, for several reasons. If the record contains a large amount of information, you can reduce

confusion by displaying only those items which are currently needed. If your records are a mixture of confidential and public information, you could then limit the amount of information displayed to that appropriate to a particular person. (For instance, in our membership records system it may be desirable to limit the display of records showing the financial status of individual members, while allowing access to non-confidential information such as addresses.) Where you can access more than one set of records at the same time, for instance in transaction-based applications, you will also need to be able to see a group of associated records together.

Every package dealing with structured records provides at least one fixed format for displaying an individual record (or pairs of records, in transaction systems) on the screen. Many packages allow you to have more than one format for displaying information (though not necessarily for amending it – see Chapter 15). So far, so good.

However, it is often more convenient to list part of several records on the screen together. For instance, you may wish to see just the names of all those members available to play table-tennis this Friday, in order to see if there are enough to make up a team. It would be much more appropriate to show these names, say, one per line on the screen, rather than taking a whole screen to show each record. The example below shows a command to list all female pool players by surname.

Display for 'pool'$Interests .and. (Title='Mrs' .or. Title='Miss') Surname

Albatross
Dragon
Eagle
Fox

Figure 21 **List of selected fields of selected records**

This feature is not universally available, so it is worth thinking about whether you need it. If you do need it, it is also wise to look at the way listing is handled. If the list would occupy more than one screen, it is most helpful if the package shows the first screenful and then awaits a signal from the user before showing any more. Not all provide this facility. Some actually present the whole list in one go, so that if it contains more items than can be shown on the screen, the first items will shoot past before you can read them! Another important feature is the ability to stop the display of records or lists of records if you need to – perhaps if your selection criteria have not produced quite the results you expected.

Finally, it is useful to be able to show on the screen a report destined for printing. This will enable you to check that the format is correct before the report is printed. It may also enable you to use reporting facilities which are not otherwise accessible to screen display. This is often the case with the display of summary information. For instance, you might want to check, before going to a committee meeting, how many members the club has, how many have joined in the last month, and how many applications are currently being processed. Some packages allow you to ask for this information directly on the screen, but many only have totalling and summary information available via the reporting features. If you always have a printer available and ready to go, then it may be preferable to print the summary out and take the page to the meeting. However, if you do not always have a printer available (and the printer is more likely to go wrong than any other part of the system), then it is good to be able to show the figures on the screen instead.

Simple reporting on individual records
Quite often, you are likely to need a simple printed copy of a record as it appears on the screen. Many packages allow you to take what is known as a 'dump' of the screen, to meet that need. This is a very convenient approach, as it avoids having to take any special action to determine the format in which the information is to be printed, and the printed copy can be available immediately. An example of a *screen dump* is shown opposite. An acceptable alternative is for the package to provide a 'default' print format (that is, a standard format supplied by the system) for quick printing of individual records.

You may also want printed versions of lists of records appearing on the screen; a useful feature here is the ability to 'echo' on the printer

```
CARDBOX(U)      File = B:CLUBMRS.FIL      PRINT
Level 1 – RECORD 1 OF 3
```

Member's number: Smith01   Title Mr   Initials A.B.

Surname Smith

Add1   14 Berry Road   Add2 Parkway

Add3   SEASIDE   Postcode PL13 2HH

Date of joining 831213   Membership grade Family

Date last paymnt 831213   Amount of payment £20.00

Interests tennis bowls pool table-tennis

Figure 22 **Example of screen dump of a record**

exactly what is displayed on the screen. (This can also be very useful
if the package is not working in quite the way you think it should,
either because of some mistake on your part or because of a fault in
the package or even the computer itself.) This feature is very similar
to the ability to get a 'dump' of a complete screen. However, you
should not assume that because one is provided it follows that the
other is also available, since the former involves printing a copy of a
static display, while the latter may involve echoing on the printer a
moving or 'rolling' display.

*In this chapter, we have been concerned with the ways that infor-
mation can be displayed on the screen, whether through the display of
individual records, or through lists or reports. The production of
printed reports is the subject of the next chapter.*

10 Producing formal reports

In addition to displaying information on the screen, you will also want to print formatted reports. Where these are to be circulated widely, especially outside your organisation, you will need good facilities for controlling the layout of these reports. You may also want to include some items of data in personalised letters and on address labels.

Formatted reports

There are two common requirements for printing formatted reports on structured information. The first is to produce tabular reports. You might, for instance, want a printed list of all payments made by members in the last month, showing the purpose of each payment and the date paid. You would probably want to show the information about each member on a separate line of the printed report. Almost all packages make such a feature available, though they vary in the ease with which such reports can be set up – more on this in Chapter 16.

You may also need the ability to total numeric fields (such as the amount of each payment) over all the set of records printed. In some applications, you will need to be able to divide your records up into categories (such as membership grades in our club example) and produce totals for each category (usually called sub-totals) as well as for all the records processed. You may also need to count the occurrences of particular values (such as the number of payments made by each kind of credit card and by cheque, as a cross-check against the dockets received). Totals are almost always available where columnar reports are provided; sub-totals are common, while counts are rare.

For sub-totals to be accumulated, the information must first be sorted or indexed in category order. In the membership example, the category of membership determines the scope of each sub-total, while the item to be totalled might be the subscription paid, or the value of each payment. The records would therefore need to be sorted so that all those relating to one membership grade appear together. If you need this facility, then even if you do not otherwise need to sort records, you will need to ensure that the sorting facilities are adequate for producing sub-totals.

In some situations, you may need more than one level of sub-totalling. For instance, in a firm with regional offices, the central personnel department may need to print reports which sub-total information by region and by department within region. As with most features, greater flexibility in this respect is likely to be balanced by the complexity experienced in setting up the reports – more on this in Chapter 16. You may also pay a substantial time penalty, since the package may have to carry out a lengthy sorting process in order to provide three or four levels of sub-total. While sophisticated totalling and sub-totalling features are quite widely available, the ability to count the number of records which fall into particular categories is less common. Some packages allow you to name temporary fields which can hold the values of such counts, while a few explicitly cater for counting and tabulating.

In addition to specifying the information to be printed, you will also want to have some control over the layout of the report. Most packages provide the ability to specify the position of fields on the page, to control the overall layout of each page, and to specify the arrangements for printing totals, sub-totals and other calculated information. You may usually also specify information to be printed at the head and foot of each page. An example of a simple formatted report is shown overleaf.

A special instance of a formatted, printed report is a set of address labels. It is possible to buy such labels mounted on to backing sheets for use with the tractor feed mechanism available for most printers. Some packages simply allow you to use the standard reporting features to set up the appropriate printing format, while others provide options to make this specialised task easier. In either case, if you need to print labels, you should check what facilities are

DELTA Standard Report

15-12-83   Page:1

Surname	Pickup . . .	Adults	Children	Senr cits
Lang	Hilltop Bus Stand	2	0	0
Smith	Hilltop Farm	3	2	0
Smith	Sea Front	4	2	2
		9	4	2

Figure 23 **A simple formatted report**

provided, and in particular check the kinds of labels you can use.
For instance, some packages do not provide facilities to allow you to
print labels where two or three are mounted side by side across the
backing sheet.

Merging data with text
When printing formatted reports, the main purpose of including
additional text is to provide labelling information to make the
report easier to read. However, you will also often need to print
records in a form in which items are embedded in text which is
essential to the purpose of printing the record. The most common
situation in which this need arises is in the printing of 'personalised'
letters of the kind often produced by word processors. The example
opposite shows a typical template for such a letter, produced by the
Delta package. Each group of underline characters represents a
field which will be filled with information from an item in a record in
your data file.

   To print such a 'standard' letter, you need to set out the body of
the text which is to be repeated in each letter, with cues embedded
within the text showing where items from your records are to be
printed. It should be easy to include the same field in different parts
of the text. For instance, you may need to include a name in the
appropriate form in both the name-and-address heading at the top
of a letter, and in the salutation at the beginning of the letter proper.
It should not be necessary for the name to appear twice in the data
file. Most packages which offer a 'personalised letter' feature do in
fact cater for this situation.

_____   _____
_____
_____
_____
^^^^^^^^^^

Dear_____   _____,

You will remember that about a month ago I wrote to remind you that
your annual club subscription, due on_____, should be paid.
As you have not yet done so, I would be grateful if you would let me
have your subscription at once.
Yours sincerely,

Ken Woodison, Club secretary

Figure 24 **Standard letter format**

Some data management systems are, however, less flexible in
allowing for the fact that the information to be embedded in the text
may vary in length. For instance, you may wish to include in the
running text of a letter some varying information, such as the venue
for the club's next table-tennis match. This will require a different
amount of space in the letter according to whether the game is to be
played at 'The Lion' or at 'The Walmesly and Shoreditch Sports and
Leisure Centre'. Some packages require you to allow as much space
as may be needed, and do not 'wrap round' extra text on to the next
line of the letter, or close up the gap if the field is shorter than the
space allowed. As a result, you must either arrange the letter
carefully to ensure that embedded items from records always
appear on an otherwise empty line, or put up with the ugly gaps
which will result from leaving the maximum amount of space which
might be necessary.

The alternative is to accept that the data management system may
not be as flexible as a word processor, and to create the 'personalised' letters using a word processor instead. To do this may
involve creating a data file in a different format from that used in the
data management system, containing the information to be printed
in the personalised letters: we shall look more closely at this
problem in Chapter 12.

Printing unstructured information

Data management packages vary significantly in their ability to print unstructured text. Most simply place it within a report as best they can, varying considerably in their ability even to split text at word boundaries. If your information includes much text, you should make sure that you see an example of a formatted report which contains a reasonable quantity of text taken from stored records.

Sequencing information and making selections

The facilities available for selecting groups of records and for sequencing them are usually the same whether for screen display or for reporting. In some packages, however, only more limited facilities are available when printing, and you should check this. The problem is particularly likely to arise where records must be sequenced by several items, such as town within county within country. If this involves physically sorting each complete record, this may take a long time.

Printed reports require appropriate formats to allow the material to be laid out neatly on the page. Reports may consist either of summary tables and lists, or of one complete page for each record; a special case of the latter is the personalised letter. Other aspects of printing will be considered in the next chapter.

11 Special problems of printing

Printers are slow devices compared with computers themselves; they are also more liable to failure. They can be very noisy. Your aim should be to arrange printing in such a way as to minimise the problems which these factors may create, using a package which helps in this respect.

Printing reports and standard letters may well take up quite a lot of the time that your data management system is in use, because printers are slow devices compared with other parts of the computer system. Typically it will take about a minute to print a page of a report or letter. The data management package should therefore provide features which will help to ensure that users make the minimum number of mistakes, and that printing interferes as little as possible with your other work.

The most common cause of mistakes when trying to print is the availability of the printer – or rather the lack of it! Some packages will not run at all unless a printer is connected, which can be very inconvenient. Others make no special provision for checking that the printer is available, but just stop if it is not, which is probably worse. This difficulty usually arises because your computer is using an operating system which cannot send a message to the program that the printer is not available, so a program must just wait until the printer is connected. The package can call your attention to this problem by displaying a message that it is checking that the printer is available. Then, if nothing happens, there is a fair chance that you will realise your mistake, and connect the printer.

Apart from this bugbear, there are four main aspects to the twin needs to avoid mistakes and to avoid interference between printing and other tasks. Ideally, you should have the ability to:

- carry out other tasks on the computer while it is printing;
- check beforehand the material to be printed;
- set up the printing so that it does not need any intervention;
- ensure that printing which requires special stationery can be controlled, to minimise the need to change stationery.

The ability to print a report while you are working on other tasks on the computer, whether within the data management system or using some other program, depends on the relationship between the package and the operating system on your computer. Clearly, the first essential is that the operating system be capable of carrying out two tasks at once. However, the data management system must work in such a way as to allow you to leave the printing task and start on another. If you then want to run a different program, such as a word processor, that may be quite a straightforward matter. However, the data management package may not make it possible to carry out another operation within that package; for instance, you may not be able to list records from the holiday bookings file on the screen while you are printing subscription records. You will almost certainly not be able to access, in any other task, records from the data file which is currently being printed. If this could be a problem, or if your operating system cannot carry out two tasks at once, then it may be worth having extra memory for your printer. This enables you to exploit the faster processing speed of the computer, by transferring all the information to be printed into the printer's own memory. The printer can then get on with the printing while freeing the computer for other tasks. The computer is tied up only for the time it takes to process your report and pass it to the printer's memory, not for the (usually much longer) time taken to print it out.

Checking the printing before you begin is made easier if you can first display the report on the screen. But the printed version of a report will often use wider margins than can easily be displayed on the screen, so it is also helpful if there is an easy way to print a page or two for a final check of a long report, before going ahead. One package allows you to change very easily from printing on single sheets to printing on continuous paper, and when printing on single sheets gives you the option to abandon the printing after each sheet. So you can print a page or two with the system set to use single sheets, and then, if all is correct, abandon that printing and re-start after telling the system that you now have continuous paper available. However, even if you check carefully before you start, problems may arise during the course of a printing task. The package should, therefore, also allow you to stop printing in mid-flight.

The package should allow you to leave the printer to get on with its task, without expecting any intervention while printing a report. A few packages expect confirmation that each sheet has been correctly printed, but this is rare. Provided you have some appropriate method of feeding paper (one which does not require manual intervention), and provided the package works correctly in harness with your printer and its paper feeding mechanism(s), this should not be a problem. You should check this second point, since not all packages can cope with all printers and all methods of feeding paper.

For some printing tasks, you may need to use special stationery. The most obvious example is labels, for printing names and addresses, etc., since this is usually much less error-prone than printing envelopes directly. Another example is the printing of special forms, such as invoices, delivery notes, orders, which are used in a variety of applications. You may also want to use headed paper for personalised letters, as well as ordinary plain paper for reports. If your headed paper is supplied mounted on stationery which can be fed through the printer's tractor feed mechanism, then the problem will be limited to the need to batch up each kind of printing, so that you are not continually changing the stationery mounted in your printer.

You may wish to use a printer attachment which can feed single sheets of paper automatically (usually called a sheet feeder) when printing on headed notepaper. You will then also need to ensure that you are not continually changing from printing on headed paper to other kinds of printing, since this will require a change of paper feeding mechanism as well as a change of stationery. Some people who face this problem choose to have two printers: a high quality daisy-wheel printer with a sheet feeder for headed paper and for plain sheets for reports which must be of the highest possible standard; and a cheap matrix printer with a tractor feed for other work, including the printing of address labels. This has the additional advantage of giving protection against the failure of one printer.

In either of these circumstances, it is important to make sure that the package can indeed 'batch up' printing so that it can take place at a time appropriate to your situation. A system which must produce an invoice on paper each time an order is entered could become extremely irksome in practice, especially if your invoices are produced on pre-printed stationery.

In this chapter, we have been concerned with the pitfalls and special needs of printing, especially where special stationery is needed. In addition to straightforward printed output, you may also need to produce printed output of a quality usually associated with word processing, or graphical output, or to carry out additional processing of your information on another computer: these subjects are discussed in the next chapter.

12 Communicating with other packages and computers

*In some applications, it is necessary to process your information in ways which the data management package may not be able to provide: you may need **graphical output, modelling facilities, or extensive word processing**. If this is so, you will probably have to translate your records into a special **transport format**, to pass them between the data management package and other processing programs.*

Communication between a data management package and another program on the same or another computer is rarely easy, and should therefore be undertaken only when essential. So in what circumstances might you need to do such a thing? The general answer is, when the other program has facilities you need but cannot get within the data management system, or when other people need the information for use elsewhere.

A common requirement is the need for more extensive word processing facilities than those provided in the data management package. Another is to be able to draw graphs based on the data. A third possibility is that you may want to use some of the figures to model future activity, in a spreadsheet or modelling package. Some packages, often called 'integrated packages', try to provide all these facilities under one umbrella. So far, however, it has not proved possible to do this without significant loss in facilities, or in speed, or in the size of records or files which can be handled by the data management features. This may change, but there are grounds for supposing that inherent difficulties lie in the way. This question is discussed further in Chapter 27.

If you do need to transfer information between two packages, you will almost certainly have to copy the data file into an alternative format. The need to process information quickly usually means that, within a package, the data is stored in a special format (often called an *internal format*) understood only by that particular package. To get information to another package, your data must be translated into a format which the other package can understand. Frequently, the package to which you are transferring information will also have its own internal format, and therefore another translation must then take place. You will see that the intermediate format is needed only to act as a transport medium, as a kind of 'lingua franca' understood by both packages.

There are several forms of 'lingua franca': some packages understand them all, others only one. The most common is the so-called *comma-delimited format*, in which the value of each field in a record is separated by a comma, and the end of each record terminated by the two characters generated when you press the RETURN key on your computer keyboard. This is the format used by the *Mail/Merge* facility in the *WordStar* word processing package, when creating personalised letters. You may also encounter a 'fixed' format in which each field always occupies the maximum amount of space ever needed by that field (the reading program then knows which field is which just by counting columns along the record). Finally, the DIF™ format (devised by a company called Software Arts in the US) is commonly used by spreadsheets.

Whatever the format of the transport file, you should also consider whether you need to select parts of the information for transfer, or to transfer it in any particular order. Sometimes the facilities for selection and ordering are either more limited or slower in these circumstances than when reporting within the package. Speed can be a general problem with transporting records – some systems are very slow at importing and exporting information, taking over an hour to transfer 1,000 records. On floppy disk systems, the amount of information you can transfer may be limited by whether you can have two data disks available at the same time; if not, then the file to be transferred may occupy no more than half a floppy disk.

If you are passing information between packages on the same computer, it may well suffice to transfer information using a file format understood by them both. However, if you need to pass information between two computers, you will encounter additional problems. These relate to the communication, at both the physical level and the logical level, between the two computers, and are beyond the scope of this book. Some of the sources of help and advice mentioned in the Appendix will aid you in this area.

In most circumstances, you will not need to concern yourself with transferring information between the data management package and other programs. However, if you need specially flexible word processing features applied to your data, or if you need to draw graphs or use spreadsheet modelling, you may need to extract information from the data management package and pass it to another program for further processing. Some suites of packages allow you to do this within a single environment, with the copying facilities an integral part of the system. The alternative is to use separate programs for each function, transferring information between them in a 'lingua franca' understood by both packages. If this transfer is taking place not only between two packages but also between two computers, you need to consider a variety of other questions as well.

13 Questions of quantity and speed

*Once you have decided what results you want from your infor-
mation, and what kinds of processing you need to do to get those
results, you are in a position to estimate **how much information** you
have, and the likely constraints on **speed of processing**.*

If you were to take a motoring trip through the Himalayas, you
would not expect to do as well in a compact car as you would in a big
saloon – or, even better, a jeep. And you would not pack three
suitcases to take with you on a hiking holiday – you would travel
light. The same kind of logic applies to 'sizing' a data management
application: it's 'horses for courses'. If you need to store hundreds
of thousands of records, and to process them in many different
ways, a microcomputer with a simple card-index-like data management system may not be powerful enough for your needs. On the
other hand, you don't need a large mainframe and a full data base
management system to handle a few thousand records with a simple
structure.

People are inclined to think that sizing is important only in
judging how large a computer you need, but this is not the case.
Data management packages will usually take no more than a few
seconds to find a record in even a very large file, provided you are
searching on the primary key. On the other hand, packages vary
tremendously in the time they take to sort a set of records into a
different order; this can take anything from a few minutes to several
hours for files of the same size and structure. So an important aspect
of choosing a package will be to get some feel for how much
information you have, and to identify the critical processes for
which speed is essential.

Counting the information you want to store and assessing its volume may be easy in some circumstances. For instance, in our club membership example, the secretary knew how many members there were, and how many holiday bookings are taken each year. In Part 4 we shall see examples of how these numbers are used to assess needs for storage; it is just a matter of simple arithmetic. The first step is to decide what you want to store, and in what formats. Then, allow one character of storage for each character in each character field in your record, characters equal to half the length of each numeric field for numbers, and three characters for each date. The result gives you roughly the length of each record if the records are to be fixed in length, and the maximum length of each record in a package which stores information in variable format.

If the figure comes out to more than 1,000 characters, your choice of package will be considerably restricted, since only a few allow larger records. You should also beware of assuming that a field may be of any length; most packages do not allow you to have a field which exceeds the width of the screen, and many restrict you to 70 characters or even fewer.

You may find it harder to predict the number of records you may eventually want to store. Some packages oblige you to say at the outset, when a file is created, how many records it will contain; if you ever need to exceed that number, you must copy out the whole file to some kind of transport format, and copy it back. Such a process could take many hours with a large file. As we saw in Chapter 12, you may also have to copy information out to a plain text file if you want to pass information to some other package such as a word processor. So while many packages make great play of their ability to communicate with other programs, you should make sure that the time it takes to do the transfer is acceptable to you.

Sorting records into order is another potentially lengthy process. Those packages which allow you to index on many different fields can completely avoid the need to sort, and indexing is much quicker than sorting. When printing reports, however, you may have to carry out a physical sort. For instance, many packages allow you only to index on one field at a time, although they do allow you to sort using several fields. So if you have information which you want sorted by county, and within county by town, or if you wanted to sub-total, say, acreage within town within county, you may be forced to carry out a physical sort.

Finally, another common bottleneck is printing. Before you buy your system, you should also try and get some feel for the amount of printing you will need to do, and then make sure that you buy a printer which is fast enough to cope comfortably (because you will have underestimated initially, and also your needs will grow).

In each of these areas, you should beware of thinking that because the package seems fast when it is demonstrated, it will work fast when processing your records. Most dealers, and those manning stands at exhibitions, use a demonstration version of the package, which can take no more than fifteen or twenty records. (This is in part an attempt by the supplier to prevent dealers selling demonstration copies and pocketing the proceeds.) Almost any package will seem fast when processing such a small number of records.

It is well worth checking to see if any published timings exist for packages you are considering, since some of the computer magazines publish such tests. Another good source of information about times is the experience of people who are already using the package. If you ask the potential supplier for the names of some existing users, you will obviously be given the names of satisfied customers. Nevertheless, in this as in many other areas, even contented users can be a mine of information. They can help you to assess the package's strengths and weaknesses better than you can hope to do from short demonstrations at exhibitions and in dealers' showrooms. (You should, however, also remember that because a package fits someone else's needs exactly, it will not necessarily be an appropriate package for your applications. Contented users are also likely to be addicted to their own system!)

It is, however, a mistake to concentrate too much on time, tempting though this may be, since it is a quantifiable item in the midst of so many qualitative features. Sorting speed matters only if you plan to do a lot of sorting, or if your system will become very busy very quickly. It is especially important to distinguish between tasks which are carried out while you are actively using the computer, and tasks which you can leave to tick over quite happily while you do something else. Unless your computer is very busy, you can usually allow some tasks to take a long time, provided they can be left to run on their own, at night or over the weekend. It is important, however, to check that tasks which can be run without intervention can safely be left entirely alone. For instance, if the package insists that a printer be connected, or does not allow you to suppress printing, you may be unable to leave it running for fear of mechanical problems such as a jam in the printer's paper feed mechanism.

Before choosing a data management package, you will need to check the amount of information you need to store and the speed with which you need to process it. You should make sure that the system is quick to carry out tasks which will involve you in interaction with the computer. It may matter less if the system is a bit slow to carry out tasks which do not need supervision and can therefore be run out of office hours.

14 Creating record formats

*Your needs for processing should dictate what information you decide to store. Having decided that, you will then have to go through the process of telling the system about the **record format** needed to store your information. This format will be used by the system as the basic description of your information. It may also determine the way the record is displayed on the screen; alternatively, you may be able, or be obliged, to create a **screen layout** of your own choosing. If each record contains a lot of information, or your records contain confidential items, you may also need **alternative formats** for displaying your records.*

Earlier chapters in this section have been directly concerned with your requirements for handling information. The next three chapters deal with the supporting activities needed. You can think of it as being a bit like running a car – the real object is to get from A to B, but in order to make sure the car does not break down on the way you have it regularly serviced. In just the same way, for a data management system to be of value, it must provide good facilities for entering information, and for keeping it complete and accurate. These activities are obviously not ends in themselves, but it is essential that they are carried out properly if the information you get out is to be useful to you. In this chapter we shall look at the facilities you need for creating record formats, and at how they are provided.

Getting started – record definition

When you first come to use a data management package, you will need to describe the format of your information to the system in order that an appropriate record format can be set up. You may also need to give information which will determine how the screen appears when you come to enter data into a record. In some systems, this information is given by the same process as the definition of data formats, in others they are two separate operations, and in yet others the screen format is determined for you by the package.

The first stage in setting up a set of records is to tell the package the number of fields and their characteristics (maximum length, type, formula for a field whose value is calculated by the package, and so on). Clearly, before you can do this you will have had to go through the analysis of your requirements discussed in Chapters 1 and 2, and continued in Chapter 23 onwards. Having done so, you should have a written specification of the form of each record in each set you require. The way in which this is communicated to the package varies quite substantially from one system to another, but there are three main approaches. In each case, the main needs are for minimum repetition of information (it should only be necessary to give the package a piece of information once), and for maximum flexibility to make changes.

In some circumstances, it may be appropriate for the package to provide you with a *default* screen format – a format which the package will use unless told otherwise. You then enter only the name, type and size of each field. This might be appropriate where you want to start with the minimum of initial effort, or where the data structure you have decided upon dictates to a large extent the way in which the information should be displayed on the screen. Quite a good compromise is to provide a default format which you can use for experimenting and testing the other aspects of record definition, while allowing you to describe a tailor-made screen layout later if needed. Several packages provide this combination; the default format which would be used by *dBASEII* for our club membership record is shown overleaf.

If you want complete control over the layout of your information on the screen during data entry, you must be able to dictate the positioning of the items to be displayed. These include the fields themselves and any captions or prompting information associated with them, and also any other items such as lines to separate sections of the screen.

```
Memnum :                    :
Title   :                        :
Initials   :                            :
Surname :                                    :
Add1    :                                    :
Add2    :                                    :
Add3    :                                    :
Postcode:              :
Datejoin  :            :
Grade   :                        :
Datelastp:            :
Amtpayt :         :
Interests :                              :
```

Figure 25 **Default format for club membership record**

One method of specifying the positions of items for screen display is to 'draw' the layout directly on the screen. This *paint-a-screen* method involves placing the cursor in each position which will be occupied by a data item or caption, and then using special commands to indicate what is to be placed there. The simplest method, quite commonly used, is to type the name of the data item, and then use special characters such as square brackets to show the length of the data item. Then, either at the same time or in a separate operation, you will be asked to enter the type of the item and any other necessary details, such as the formula if this item is to be calculated from others. Once set up, this screen format can then be printed for a final check; the format for storing the membership record in *CardBox* is shown opposite.

An alternative approach is to treat the screen as though it were a grid, usually containing 24 rows and 80 columns. The positioning of each field value, caption, etc., can then be indicated by specifying the row and column positions to be occupied by the item. Some systems simply store this information and display it only when you first try to enter records using the format. This can cost you a lot of time and effort, since, even if you have prepared the format accurately beforehand, you may not get the design perfect first or second time. Other systems take each specification as you enter it and show the resulting layout so that you can see the overall effect.

Whichever approach is used, it is sensible to design the screen

CARDBOX(F)   FILE = CLUBMRS.FMT.   SELECT FUNCTION   PRINT

```
Member's number: AAAAAAA      Title BBBBBBB      Initials CCCCCCC

Surname  DDDDDDDDDDDDDDDDDDDDDDDDDDDDDDDDDDDDDDDD

Add1  EEEEEEEEEEEEEEEEEEEE     Add2  FFFFFFFFFFFFFFFFFFFFF

Add3  GGGGGGGGGGGGGGGGGG      Postcode HHHHHHH

Date of joining IIIIII    Membership grade  JJJJJJJJJJJJJJJJJJJJJJJJJJJJJJJ

Date last payment KKKKKK     Amount of paymnt LLLLLLL

Interests  MMMMMMMMMMMMMMMMMMMMMMMMMMMMMMMMMMMMMMMM
```

E=edit screen   F=edit/create field   D=delete field   P=set print formats
EXIT: X=save file   Q=abandon edit
Enter function code:

Figure 26 **Format of *CardBox* record for club membership system**

layout on paper first. Even where the facilities are exceptionally
flexible, allowing you to move about the screen with ease and to
delete and create fields and captions at will, you are likely to get the
best results if you have made some plans first. You are also more
likely to succeed quickly if the package allows very flexible and
simple editing. At least one package on the market allows you to
delete only the most recently entered field – if you find you made a
mistake further back, then you must delete all the intervening
layout.

Alternative formats
Quite often, you will have two or even three sets of records which
you want to keep separate, but which are nevertheless very similar
in format. It can therefore be very helpful to be able to copy a
format and then edit the copy. This facility becomes almost essential if the system does not allow you to alter the format in which a
data file is stored – perhaps to add a field or two, or to delete fields –
once information has been entered into it.

In some circumstances, you may need to protect your information from unauthorised access. You may want to protect a whole file, or to allow people to view part of each record but not the confidential items, or to view some records but not others. Or you may want to allow people to view records but not change them. Some packages allow you to have several formats for the same file, which can be thought of as providing alternative 'windows' on to your records. In such circumstances, you also need some way to ensure that each person using the system has access only to the appropriate facilities.

This restriction is usually implemented by using some form of password, so that a user must know the correct 'secret code' in order to get at a particular file or at a particular view of it. Passwords are only as trustworthy as those who use them, so they can never be completely foolproof. On the other hand, they tend to be more convenient than the alternative approach (which is the only one possible in some packages) of keeping separate sets of disks, and locking up those containing versions of the file to which access is limited. This second approach also limits flexibility, since a person whose access is restricted sees only a partial **copy** of the main file, and cannot then be responsible for keeping up to date the parts to which they do have access. However, even that constraint is more flexible than the situation where only one format is provided, or where every format must include a reference to every field in the record.

To set up a data management system, you must first define the formats of the sets of records to be used. You also need to decide how records are to be displayed on the screen. Packages vary substantially in the flexibility they give, both to set up your own formats and to change them once set up. Changing a record definition after data has been entered into the file can be a major exercise, and this point should be checked carefully. Once the data files are ready to receive records, you can then set about entering information, the subject of the next chapter.

15 Creating and amending records

*The value of your results will be only as great as the **accuracy and timeliness of the information** you put in. The system can improve accuracy by providing good facilities for **data validation**, and by minimising the amount of information entered.*

Entering and storing records

In the previous chapter, we were concerned with setting up complete files, and with the ways in which such files could be protected from unauthorised access. In this chapter we shall look at the entry of information into files, and at the requirements for ensuring that information in individual records is accurate and is not tampered with by those not authorised to do so.

There are two major aspects to consider here: what facilities do you need to make it easy to keep your records comprehensive and accurate, and how should these facilities be provided in order to ensure that they are effective? In most circumstances, there is a trade-off between power of function and ease of use (we shall look more closely at this in Chapter 18). For instance, the need to keep your records accurate suggests that any help a package can give you in checking the correctness of the data would be very valuable. On the other hand, such checking may take quite a time to set up, and may only be worthwhile it if your records are themselves complex or lengthy, or if their precise accuracy is of great importance.

Accuracy of information can be checked in a number of ways. At the simplest level, a field that is supposed to contain only numbers must never contain letters. If this should happen, not only would the record contain inaccurate information, but also any calculations on such a value would fail. Any package which stores numbers differently from items which may contain any character should, and in most cases will, prevent you from entering letters in numeric fields. Most packages with a special date format prevent the entry of invalid dates.

It is also common for the package to prevent you exceeding the maximum length of the field. Another useful but less common feature is the ability to specify a pattern which the value of a field must match. A good example would be the code for UK vehicle licensing plates that we looked at in Chapter 4, where any vehicle registration number must conform to a fixed pattern of letters and numbers of not more than seven characters.

So much for checking information that is entered into a field. It can also be important to ensure that **some** information is entered, that is, that a field may not be left empty. Some packages refuse to store a record lacking values for fields which you have designated mandatory.

If there is to be any benefit in checking that information is being entered correctly, the system should take account of the fact that the person entering the information may not be looking at the screen very much while doing so. The more helpful the system, the more likely this is to be so. For instance, most packages allow the user to move through the record one field at a time using a single key. A touch-typist or data preparation clerk will therefore look mostly at the original material being typed (though a two-finger typist will look alternately at keyboard and original data). The system should therefore issue an audible warning when an error occurs.

It is, however, possible to go too far in this direction: at least one widely available package 'bleeps' whenever keyboard entry fills a field completely, which is the norm in records with a very regular format. (The bell can be turned off, but you then lose the audible warning in situations when the system is not 'crying "Wolf!" ').

These considerations apply to making sure that data entered from the keyboard is valid. Accuracy is also enhanced if the minimum amount of information is entered in that way: as far as possible, the hard work of data entry should be done by the system. Firstly, where any item has the same value across a number of records, it should be entered only once. For instance, in some systems, you can define a field in each record which will contain the date at which the record was first entered – a particularly useful feature where you are entering records such as a series of invoices all to be issued on the same day.

Another way to avoid entering the same data repeatedly is to 'echo' the value of a field from the value of the same field in the previous record. This allows you to enter quickly and accurately several records which have one or more items in common – for instance, several members of our club might have the same set of interests. Some packages allow you to echo whole records, though this is rarely as useful as echoing individual fields. However, the ability to 'echo' values from other records should be used with caution, since it is also important not to store duplicate information, because it is difficult to keep all the copies up to date. For instance, you would be unwise to apply the same approach to keeping records about members of families and their addresses. This question, with its implications for structure, will be discussed further in Part 4.

Where the same values are found over and over again throughout a set of records, a table or reference facility is very helpful. For example, if the interests which could be entered in a club member's record were limited to fifteen or twenty items, it might be better to have a short code for each one, and to store a table which related the code to the full name of the interest. Table-tennis could then be stored as TT, shark fishing as SF, and so on. When a member's record is displayed on the screen, the system matches the code with the full name before displaying the record. During data entry, you should have the option of entering a code when you are certain of the abbreviation, or of interrogating the system to discover what legal codes and corresponding interests existed in the system, or of entering the full name and having it stored in its abbreviated form.

Such a facility can also help in keeping up-to-date information which may change fairly regularly. For example, in the club membership records example, there were a few subscription rates which apllied to the whole membership. Rather than entering the value of the subscription due in each record, it is better to have a code for the membership grade, and a separate table relating grades with subscription rates. Then, when membership rates change, only that one table needs to be altered rather than every member's record.

So much for data values which commonly recur. The second aspect of minimising keyboard entry concerns field values which depend on the values of other fields. These may be of two kinds: they may need to be calculated once and then remain static, or to be recalculated each time the record is changed. For example, the VAT or sales tax due on a sale is calculated once and then remains static, since it depends on the net value of the sale and the rate of tax in force when the invoice is issued. Even if the rate of tax changes before the invoice is paid, the tax is not recalculated.

But in other circumstances, the value of a field may need to change if the value of the fields used to calculate it changes. For example, we saw in Chapter 4 that it is better to store a person's date of birth and to calculate his or her age when necessary, rather than to store the age (which will change with every birthday). Nevertheless, it will often be preferable to display the person's age on the screen, or use it in a comparison. Age can, of course, be calculated by comparing the date of birth with the current date, and will change as the current date changes. It therefore saves effort and possible inaccuracy to specify 'age' as a calculated value, which is to be recalculated whenever the record is retrieved.

Most packages achieve this result by allowing you to define a field in each record which will hold the results of such a calculation; the calculation is made when the record is first entered, and repeated whenever the record is retrieved. Alternatively, the field may be a 'dummy' item, used only for display; the system stores the formula to be used in the calculation (only once, not once per record), and uses it to construct the value to be displayed on the screen, used in a selection test, or reported on the printer. This approach saves the disk space which the stored field would have taken in each record.

Keeping information up to date
There are two main ways of ensuring that information is kept up to date. Records may be retrieved individually for editing on the screen. An alternative is to construct instructions to enable the system to change records in the desired way, simply by applying those instructions without your intervention.

If you need to make an amendment which is specific to an individual record, such as changing the address of a person who has moved house, you would recall the record to the screen and enter the changes. Usually the easiest way to do this is to type in the new entry over the old. Some packages, however, do not allow you to do this: they require you to enter the name or number of the field to be changed on the bottom line of the screen, and then to enter the new information in the same way. This approach is rather awkward to use. Whichever method is used, the package should check that the new data is correct before replacing the old.

Validation of changes made in records should include all the checks made when data is entered for the first time, but there are some extra checks which you may wish to apply. For instance, some fields should never be changed if the information is to remain correct; a membership number is one example, a customer's account number is another. Most fields which are derived from others, such as the tax on an invoice, should not normally be changed either. Such safeguards should be built into the record format. Other items, such as a person's salary, might be restricted so that they can be changed only by someone with the correct authorisation. Such protection would need to be enforced, perhaps by a password mechanism similar to that needed for data entry.

On occasion, you will want to delete records altogether. It should go without saying that it is especially important for the system to check that the correct record is being deleted, at least by requesting confirmation from the keyboard. In some circumstances deletion should not be permitted: for instance, you should not be able to delete a master record when there are associated transaction records in existence.

In addition to making changes to individual records, you will sometimes want to make changes to a group of records. For instance, you might want to change the price of all products which use some component which has increased in price. Or you might want to enter a list of membership numbers for people who have paid their subscription, and have the system amend each record accordingly. If a large number of subscriptions are paid over a short period, this approach would be quicker than retrieving each record individually.

Packages vary in the extent to which they can carry out such tasks. The first kind of 'automatic update', in which a simple formula is applied to one field in all or selected records, is quite common. The second, in which the system must compare a list of identifiers each of which will match only one record, and carry out the correct change each time, is less common. It is comparable to the kind of facility which transaction processing packages provide for automatically associating transaction records with master records. This is no coincidence, since the operation involves *posting* updates to master records, in a way which mimics some features of structured data storage using flat format files. If this kind of approach meets your needs, the most important feature is the ability to check carefully that the correct records are updated. For example, there must be some provision for the situation where the list of updates refers to a record which does not exist in the master set.

In either form of automatic update, it is vital to check carefully that updates are applied in the right way to the intended records. You should always take the precaution of copying data files regularly. You should make a point of doing this before a major updating operation, such as an automatic update or deletion. Then, if mistakes are made, you will still be able to revert to the state of your information before the changes were made.

The package can help considerably in enabling you to recover in the event of failure by keeping a record of what changes have been made: such a record is sometimes called an audit trail. These precautions are particularly important with automatic updating, since you may not have any manual records to fall back on (as you may have when information is amended from the keyboard). If the automatic facilities include record deletion, then some kind of explicit audit trail is essential. It is also vital if there is any danger of information being deliberately falsified (for instance where sizeable sums of money are involved).

A simple audit trail involves taking a copy of all transactions, either to a separate file or to the printer. A more sophisticated approach, called journalling, records the changes in such a way that, should the system go wrong while the changes are being made, they can automatically be re-applied later, when you are sure the problems have been solved.

To gain accurate and up-to-date results from your system, you must ensure that the information it contains is accurate and up to date. The data management package should help in this by checking data as it is entered, and by providing facilities to calculate fields itself where this is appropriate. In the next chapter, we look at ways of maintaining complete files, and at setting up formats for report printing and record selection.

16 Maintaining data and work files

*The importance of keeping records up to date is obvious; it is also important to maintain complete files properly, by taking **security copies** regularly. The package can help by providing good file handling features. You will also need to maintain the work files in which the package may store report formats, selection criteria, and sets of commands to be executed automatically.*

Maintaining data files

So far in these chapters on maintenance we have been concerned with the problems of setting up individual records and keeping them up to date. This section deals with the problems of handling complete files in such a way as to keep the whole data management system up to date. You will as a minimum need to be able to delete complete files, and to copy them as a security precaution. These activities can of course be carried out within the operating system. It is, however, much better if they are available within the package, since it then means that you are carrying out all the activities relating to the data management system under the one umbrella. This may not be possible on a twin-disk-drive system, since the package must enable you to change disks and to run without any program disk in the machine. This is the only way to copy a large data file, for which there would not be enough space on the program disk, or where the data file occupies more than half the data disk. If the facilities available include the preparation of disks for use in storing data files, so much the better.

In some circumstances, you will want more powerful facilities still. For instance, you may need very powerful word processing features, involving copying a data file into an external format, branching out to run the word processing program, and returning to the data management system. In these circumstances, it is helpful if the data management system has the 'hooks' into the operating system to permit this to take place as an automatic sequence. This is almost essential if the system is to be operated by relatively naive users, but such an approach can in any case be a great saver of time, and prevent many trivial but irritating errors.

Creation and maintenance of report formats

Many of the considerations which apply to designing screen layouts also apply to the design of report formats. In particular, the three different approaches – a default format, the paint-a-screen technique, and the specification of row and column co-ordinates – are also used to specify report formats. A 'default' format for producing columnar reports (as distinct from personalised letters and the like) can be especially helpful. Where this is provided, the user is usually asked only for the names of fields to be included in the report; the maximum permitted lengths of the fields determine the report layout. However, you will often want to produce your own layout. An excellent compromise is to provide a default format which can subsequently be edited by the user, to 'tweak' it into the exact shape required. An example of a simple layout, which could subsequently be tailored if necessary, follows. (The report resulting from using this layout was shown in Chapter 10.)

Whatever the method used to describe the report format, it must be possible to edit the format later, to hone it to the required result. Without such a feature, you cannot produce several similar versions of a report without re-entering the specification from scratch each time. These points cannot be emphasised too strongly. Salesmen often emphasise the merits of screen layout, and of course this is important. In practice, however, you still need plenty of printed reports, in greater variety of format than is commonly used on the screen.

Many packages do not make it easy to set up any necessary sub-totals and totals, and to define the conditions under which the system is to start printing on a new page. It should be possible to define separately the items which are to be sub-totalled, the items which are to cause a sub-total to be printed out and reset, and the

DELTA Report Definition: PICK1512

Item No.	Item Type	Fld No.	Spaces Before	LFeeds After	Start Pos.	Fld Len	No. Dec	Ed It	Text
1	T	T	29	1	1	21	0		DELTA Standard report
2	T	D	0	0	1	10	0		
3	T	T	54	0	1	5	0		Page:
4	T	P	0	2	1	6	0		
5	T	T	0	0	1	20	0		Surname
6	T	T	3	0	1	20	0		Pickup....................
7	T	T	3	0	1	6	0		Adults
8	T	T	3	0	1	8	0		Children
9	T	T	3	1	1	9	0		Senior citizens
10	T	T	0	1	1	79	0		^−
11	D	4	0	0	1	20	0	2	
12	D	22	3	0	1	20	0		
13	D	15	3	0	1	6	0		
14	D	16	3	0	1	8	0		
15	D	17	3	1	1	9	0		
16	4	T	0	1	1	79	0		^=
17	4	T	0	0	1	20	0		^
18	4	T	3	0	1	20	0		^
19	4	15	3	0	1	6	0		
20	4	16	3	0	1	8	0		
21	4	17	3	2	1	9	0		

Figure 27 **Standard report format**

items which are to cause a new page to be started. It should also be easy to ensure that the date file is in the correct order for these specifications to have the desired effect. (In principle, the system should be able to ensure that this is done, but in practice very few packages achieve this degree of sophistication.)

Stored selections
In some applications, you will want to carry out the same selection tests on your files many times. Many packages oblige you to store such selection criteria before you can implement them; on the whole it is better to have the choice about whether they are stored or not. However, whether storing is optional or mandatory, it is helpful to be able to edit the criteria, and to edit a copy where you want to produce an effect on an existing set of tests.

The ways in which the criteria may be stored vary widely. Some packages show a copy of the record format on the screen, and allow you to enter the values or range of values to which the selected records must conform. An example of this approach follows.

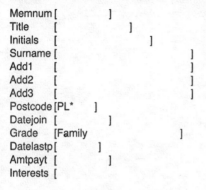

```
Memnum [              ]
Title     [                ]
Initials  [                    ]
Surname [                          ]
Add1    [                          ]
Add2    [                          ]
Add3    [                          ]
Postcode [PL*     ]
Datejoin [          ]
Grade   [Family                    ]
Datelastp[        ]
Amtpayt  [          ]
Interests  [                                                    ]
```

Figure 28 **Form-filling to specify selection criteria**

This approach provides a nice, simple method of entering the tests but makes it hard to specify that any one criterion, or some other combination, is to be met. So you must usually have the records which meet all the given criteria. A more flexible approach, but perhaps harder to use because it involves remembering more, is the command method used in the example which follows.

.Display for 'pool'$Interests .and. (Title='Mrs' .or. Title='Miss') Surname

Albatross
Dragon
Eagle
Fox

Figure 29 **Using a command to specify selection criteria**

The central task in a data management system is to get out the information you need in the correct form. In addition to those facilities which are directly necessary, you also require maintenance

*facilities to ensure that the data is and remains accurate and compre-
hensive. In the last three chapters we have looked at a variety of
requirements for maintenance functions, while continuing to note
features which make these facilities easy to use. Ease of use is not,
however, a simple touchstone to apply in practice, and in the next two
chapters we shall look explicitly at this question.*

Part 3
Implementing and using a data management system

The second part of this book has been concerned primarily with the 'what' of data management; this part is about the 'who, when and how'. We look at the needs of those who will use the system, whether it be a single individual, or several people of varying backgrounds, motivation and experience. We also look at how such a system can best be implemented: these chapters will include a discussion of possible sources of supply, as well as material on planning and training.

17 Users of the system

*In choosing and implementing a data management system, you need to be as concerned with the **people who will use the** system as with what it can do, since their co-operation can help to make the system run smoothly, while unco-operative users can make even a good system almost unworkable. Even if you are to be the only user of the system, you should consider how you would like it to behave. The **needs of users** vary according to their **experience of computing**, the **regularity** with which they will use the computer, and the **way their work is organised**. All users are likely to get on better if the data management system interacts with them in ways which are **consistent** and **appropriate**, and which make it easy to identify the **context** of the current operation.*

So far, we have been talking almost exclusively about the functions that a data management system might perform in your organisation. Another equally important question is – who would carry out the necessary tasks if such a system were introduced? This will certainly have a substantial impact on the choice of system to buy and its implementation, and may influence your decision as to whether or not to have such a system at all.

It is especially important to involve everyone who may be concerned with the project as early as possible, and to take their needs and experience into account. This is not only right, it is expedient too. First, user co-operation is essential if a system is to run smoothly, especially at the beginning, when every system has teething troubles. Second, if you are transferring from an existing manual system, the people who are currently doing the job will have

113

a lot of knowledge and expertise, much of it not made explicit or written down, which needs to be incorporated into the new system. To ignore this is to court disaster.

Deciding who is to be involved

In some circumstances, this question will answer itself. In others, you will need to think carefully about who is to use the system and who is not. It is usual to assume that younger people adapt better to new technology, but in my experience age is not significant in itself: it is better to look for adaptability and enthusiasm without worrying too much about dates on birth certificates. It is also important that those involved should be committed to solving the problem, and if new methods are to be used they need to be committed to the success of the new project. Sometimes people who have been 'getting by' in a job for a long time find it hard to see what the problems are, or to appreciate the need for change. In such circumstances they may feel threatened by plans for new methods, and regard the plans as a reflection on their ability to do the job. This argues that another important factor is a willingness to see change as having potential for good, rather than being a threat or a nuisance.

It should also be accepted that, especially in the early stages of any project, there are bound to be problems. If those using the system regard problems as challenges to be met, rather than hurdles at which to fall, you are much more likely to be successful. You will find the problems easier to solve if those using the system are methodical, for instance in keeping a record of their actions and of any problems that arise.

However co-operative and adaptable you and your colleagues are, you will of course succeed more easily if the system is easy to use. This means that the package should make it easy for users to get things right, by providing an appropriate environment in which they can work. This comment extends, of course, to the way in which the system has been set up for your particular applications. This applies whether you are the only user, who sets up, maintains and uses the package, or whether you (or someone else) are responsible for setting up the system for others to use. If you are the only user, there is a real temptation to ignore many precautions which you would take on behalf of others, and to use as many short-cuts as possible.

On the whole, you are unlikely to find that this pays off in time, energy and perhaps money, even in the short term – more will be said about this in Chapters 21 and 22.

The most important general principle about ease of use is that the package should provide you with an appropriate environment, whether you are carrying out tasks normally, or whether things are going or have gone wrong. The extent to which a system is 'forgiving' of errors, and robust in the face of actions which a system designer is most unlikely to have envisaged, is often a good guide to ease of use in a real application.

What 'an appropriate environment' is will depend partly on the kind of user and user environment we are thinking about. There are three main aspects to this question: the user's expertise and experience of the data management system, the regularity with which he or she uses it, and organisation of the environment.

The expertise and experience of the user

Clearly, for a system of any complexity, there will be a period of learning while the user becomes familiar with the system. The package can help a great deal in this: yet a system which is easy to use in the first few days may not be the most appropriate once you are expert. (It is irritating to be asked 'are you sure' for every line you type, or to be 'bleeped' at for doing quite ordinary things, once you have gained some expertise.) On the other hand, a system which is hard to learn may be very convenient once you are over the initial hurdles: those instructions which seemed so terse and incomprehensible at the beginning may later seem a model of brevity and clarity. The nature of ease of use therefore differs according to the user's level of experience of the system.

The best approach is usually to provide some prompting and error reporting on the screen, with more help available if this is explicitly requested. When you first begin to use a data management system, you will need quite a lot of prompting when doing positive things, and fairly detailed error messages when you make mistakes or when (if) the system goes wrong. This suggests that the system should provide detailed prompting, while being sufficiently economical in its use of the screen to enable prompts and task-oriented information to be displayed together. For instance, when entering information into a record, it is usually helpful to a beginner if the screen shows prompts giving the actions currently available. Such prompts should appear on the top or bottom lines of the screen, out of the way of the data display. An example of such prompts, taken from *Pearl*, follows.

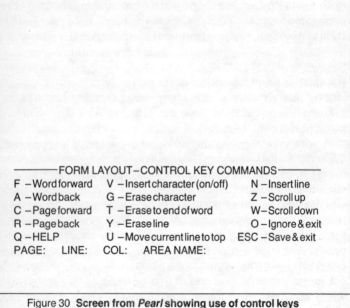

```
──────────FORM LAYOUT–CONTROL KEY COMMANDS──────────
F – Word forward      V – Insert character (on/off)    N – Insert line
A – Word back         G – Erase character              Z – Scroll up
C – Page forward      T – Erase to end of word         W – Scroll down
R – Page back         Y – Erase line                   O – Ignore & exit
Q – HELP              U – Move current line to top    ESC – Save & exit
PAGE:    LINE:    COL:    AREA NAME:
```

Figure 30 **Screen from *Pearl* showing use of control keys**

Sometimes even this level of detail will be inadequate, and you will want to seek more information. This may be provided on the screen too, most usefully by appearing when you press a 'Help' key. However, you should be wary of the apparent helpfulness of systems which show large amounts of prompt text on the screen, either as the normal situation or in response to the 'Help' key. Too much information can be as confusing as too little: in particular, if the 'Help' information is presented on a separate screen from that showing the data record, you may find it hard to remember what was displayed, when you return to the record display. The best may be for the system to provide references to its manual, so that you can look up the information you need.

Once you are familiar with the system, you will need less prompting. It should be possible to reduce the level of 'Help' which is normally provided. Ideally, you should be able to change the system so that it gives you this reduced level of 'Help' permanently, rather than having to request this each time the system is started up. In systems which are used by more than one person, the package should be able to provide the level of prompting appropriate to each individual user; however, this degree of flexibility is rare. (And beware of systems which judge for themselves how expert you are.) Even when you have reduced the prompting available, you should still be able to go back to a higher level of prompting or get extra information on demand. This allows you to ask for extra help when using parts of the system with which you are not familiar.

A good system may also play a part in the actual learning process. We look at this question more closely in Chapter 21.

So far, these comments have assumed that the screen help comes with the package. Similar observations apply to those packages which allow you to tailor the appearance of the package in a more fundamental way. Some systems have facilities which you can use to set up an environment, for yourself or for others, which relates precisely to the functions you want to carry out. Where an item in a general purpose list of options might read 'enter records', a tailored list might read 'add new consultation records to patient file'. Or when you press the 'Help' key, you may be able to get information specific to your application rather than general package help. Packages vary considerably, not only in the facilities they offer for tailoring, but in the ease with which these features can be used.

Regularity of use
The needs of those using a system all day every day differ from those of people who use it only occasionally. A package of any complexity

is like a human language: its use must be practised if you are to stay fluent. The needs of occasional users have a lot in common with those of novices, in that they may need a fair amount of prompting, but by contrast they may prefer to ask for this rather than get it automatically. They are also likely to need more summary information to remind them of points of detail which become automatic only when you are using a system regularly and intensely. Such summary information helps occasional users to get back more quickly to the level of expertise they have at their peak of usage.

There are various ways in which such summary information can be provided. The system may make summaries available on the screen, in the same way as the detailed prompting we talked about earlier. For instance, you may see the action of any special keys represented at the bottom of the screen, or on a separate small display provided for this purpose. These representations change as the function keys change for use in different parts of the system. Alternatively, a summary of facilities and their methods of use may be provided on a reference sheet or card. The example which follows shows two pages from the reference card which comes with the *Delta* package.

Selection/sort/extract

Entered in form – FIELD · OPERATOR · FIELD/CONSTANT

Operators		Character	Date	Numeric
Equal	EQ	Y	Y	Y
Not equal	NE	Y	Y	Y
Less than	LT	N	Y	Y
Greater than	GT	N	Y	Y
Less or equal	LE	N	Y	Y
Greater or equal	GE	N	Y	Y
Range	RN	Y	Y	Y
Sliding search	SS	Y	N	N
Partial field		Y	Y	N
Ignore case		Y	N	N

Up to 8 selections per definition. Connectors – AND, OR, EVERY, ANY.

Constants – numbers, characters, dates including current date, ranges.

Special selection flags –
1 Select by key at extract time.
2 Supply constant at run time.
3 Select on transaction count. Use !1 to !8.

Sort criteria

Maximum sort fields – 5.
Maximum sort field length – 100 characters.
Maximum number of records to sort – 32000.
Sort can be in ascending or descending order by field.
Character fields may be sorted on part field.

Space required

During sort – 2 × length of (sort fields – 4) × number of records/transaction to be sorted.
After sort – 4 × number of records/transactions sorted.

N.B. 1 If a record has 12 transaction entries, it will create 12 sort entries.
2 The sort work area may be on a different drive to the data file.

Extract files

Size if used for reports –
4 × number of records, transactions extracted.
N.B. This is the same file as output by the sort above.

Additional size for a browse index –
Length of sort key × number of extracted records / 100.

Processing definitions

Overall size

Maximum number of process instructions per definition – 32.
Maximum number of entries in each instruction – A destination field plus a
maximum of 6 fields, work areas or special codes.

All entries in form:

A B+C−D+E*F – **destination × value/operator/value/operator.**

Process instructions evaluated left to right, no operator precedence.

Valid values:

+,−,*,/ field(R), square root, field(I), integer, field(table) table look up.

Valid values:

Field name – any valid field name.
Work areas – ^1 to ^32.
Constants – Character # 'Joe Arts', numeric # 123. 45, date #^010185 or # ^ for
current date
Transaction count fields – !1 to !8.

Process groups:

1 Applied to header and 'top' transaction only, once only prior to type 2.
2 Applied to each extracted transaction and the header in turn.
3 Applied to header and 'bottom' transaction, once only after type 2.

Work area groups:

^1 to ^10 – zeroised prior to a group 1 process, i.e. for each new record.
^11 to ^20 – zeroised prior to each type 2 process, i.e. for each transaction.
^21 to ^32 – Not zeroised.

Tables

Maximum number of tables – 255.
Maximum entries in one table – 100.

Argument – Individual entry or range, character, date or numeric. Maximum of 15 characters.
Result – Character, date or numeric. Maximum of 40 characters.

N.B. Tables are not 'tied' to individual file definitions. They can be used anywhere.

Format in process instruction:
Field=field(table name).

Figure 31 **Part of reference card for *Delta***

Such a reference summary is especially valuable if small enough to put in a pocket or handbag. It can also be helpful, though, if the print is large enough for you to post a copy up by the computer, so that it is visible when you are using the keyboard. Alternatively, the package may provide a poster as well as a pocket summary.

Organisation of users

If the system is to be used only by one person, the responsibility for it is clear. If several people are involved (even if there is only one computer), it is important to ensure that mistakes are not caused by confusion about responsibility. A good system will make it easy to take such precautions, but these may still require discipline which a group of users will find hard to sustain.

For instance, if users share data disks, there must be some method of ensuring that particular data files are accessed only by those authorised to use them. For this to be possible, someone must have the authority to issue users with identification information and, where appropriate, passwords. In other words, the security provisions permitted by the system can only be as effective as their implementation in your organisation. Some systems will **only** work effectively if someone has sufficient control over the system to enforce discipline. For instance, it may be necessary to keep sufficient spare disk space for some utilities such as sorting programs to work. Most of these problems are common to all kinds of application, but because data management systems are likely to use large amounts of resources, especially disk space, lack of control may cause particular problems here.

Ways in which the system can help
The system itself can facilitate successful use, and enable people to recover from errors. An important factor is that the system's behaviour should be **consistent**. It should be possible to extend your picture or model of how the system works, by deducing its behaviour from the results of similar situations you have encountered before. By the same token, the package should not take a completely unexpected route when handling problems similar to those you have already met. (We call this 'the principle of minimum surprise'.)

Consistency in behaviour of the system is especially important when the user is taking a sequence of actions different from that expected by the package. For instance, if you find that, before you can complete a task, you need extra information on how it is performed, you will need to 'interrupt' the task to ask the system for the necessary details. Such an interruption should be possible, and it should always be achieved in the same way, perhaps by keeping a single special key for the purpose. It will then be easy to remember that, wherever you are in the package, you just press a particular key to interrupt the current task and get extra information.

It is also important to be able to tell whereabouts you are in a package. This may be achieved by showing a message at the top of the screen indicating the task you are currently carrying out – setting up a report, editing a file of stored commands and so on. Consistency is also important here. For instance, some packages always display one symbol when awaiting a command, and another when expecting a response as a result of acting on a command issued previously. Context information is especially valuable when the system is eliciting responses to a series of questions, where some of the answers to earlier questions may affect your subsequent answers.

Another important principle is that actions taken by the system should be appropriate to the task and the user involved. This point was briefly referred to earlier, when discussing the needs of individual users. It applies also to discriminating between different activities and situations. For instance, it is quite common to sound the computer's bell – 'bleep' – when the user's attention is needed for some message on the screen. This bleep is best used only to signal a serious error by the system or the user, or to call the user's attention to the completion of a task which the system was carrying out without intervention. One package does not use the bleep in this latter situation, but does bleep each time the user is asked to change floppy disk, even in circumstances where the user would in any case be watching the screen. The problem is compounded by the package sounding the bleep, not once, but five times! Such apparently minor points can become a source of real irritation over a long period.

The handling of errors is often a good test of the appropriateness of the package's responses. When you make a mistake (or the system makes an error), you need to know what caused the problem and how to put it right. A system will often tell you that you have made a 'syntax error' when you have made a typing mistake while entering an instruction. A good system should show the exact location of the offending character or word, explain the nature of the error (briefly, with the option to get more information on request), and offer the user the chance to put the mistake right with minimum effort. It can sometimes be extremely hard for the system designer to ensure that appropriate error and recovery information is given, for instance when the package is carrying out a complex operation – but equally this is just when you most need this help.

When deciding whether to use a data management package, it is important to consider the needs of those who will actually use the system, whether it be just one person or several. Users differ in their requirements according to whether they are novices or have been using the system for some time, and whether they are regular users or use the system only occasionally. Different approaches are suited to particular kinds of user; more about this in the next chapter. Some aspects of ease of use are affected by the type of environment concerned, and in particular by the number of users who will be involved; the question of multiple use will be discussed in Chapter 19. Whatever the user profile, it is important the system should behave in a consistent and appropriate way in every situation. In this respect, error handling is the Achilles' heel of many a package. It is also important that the system should provide contextual clues, so that you can identify the sort of task by looking at the screen. The system may be especially appropriate for use by novices, in providing training in its own use. This will affect your training requirements, as we shall see in Chapter 21. The availability of training will depend heavily on your source of supply, the subject of Chapter 20.

18 Matching users and data management packages

*Each data management package has its own **style of use**, sometimes called its **user image**; it is possible to classify these styles into three main types, those which use **menus**, those which use **commands**, and those which provide 'hooks' into a **programming language**. The appropriate approach will vary according to the **type of user**. This chapter deals with the association between types of user and styles of package.*

In the last chapter we looked at the needs of different kinds of user, in particular contrasting the needs of novice and experienced users, and of regular and occasional users. Next we look at the ways these differing needs might be met, and at the approaches used by a variety of packages.

Clearly, any package must have a mechanism whereby the user can issue instructions on how the information is to be manipulated. There are four main ways in which such instructions can be given: menus, question-and-answer, form-filling and commands. Most packages use one or two of these approaches; each has merits and drawbacks for various kinds of user and for different tasks.

Menus

A *menu* is a list of options shown on the screen; beside each menu option is a number or letter, and the appropriate number or letter is typed to indicate your choice. The standard main menu for the *Delta* package is shown opposite.

Menus provide a simple and easily-understood method of issuing instructions, and are therefore especially helpful to novice users. However, the menu should not be too long or too verbose, because

DELTA – A CompSoft DATA MANAGEMENT SYSTEM

(C) CompSoft 82 02DEC82 Licence number: 10044 1.1

CompSoft Demo Version
Internal use only

START UP
A: Configure DELTA for your computer
B: Define a DELTA file for your system

SETUP/AMEND

| C: Screen layouts | D: Select/Sort criteria | E: Process instructions |
| F: Report layouts | G: Link and Copy | H: For future use |

ACTION

I: Data entry via mask	J: Extract records	K: Process records
L: Produce reports	M: Link	N: Copy
O: Use utilities	P: Change logged file	Q: Quick report/data entry

Figure 32 **Example of a main menu – from *Delta***

it must be easily read and understood on the screen. In a powerful
system it may therefore be necessary to use several levels of menu,
with each option leading to another set of options, to reach the
appropriate part of the package.

Chains of menus have two drawbacks. The disadvantage for
novices is that they must be aware of the structure of the package,
and the location of at least the most commonly needed functions, to
know which route to follow through the set of menus. The process is
a bit like navigating on strange roads – and indeed a 'road map' of
the menus, showing the point of invocation of each function, can be
a great help, but is rarely provided. (*Delta* avoids this problem by
varying the approach according to the task; below the main menu,
there may be another menu, or the package may use question-and-
answer to elicit responses.) For a more experienced user, the
process of going through a whole sequence of menus which he or she
knows off by heart is extremely tedious. The package can avoid this
necessity by providing short-cuts, but an alternative approach may
be preferable as also being more flexible.

The package *Tomorrow's Office* (Figure 33) provides another good example of how these problems can be avoided. The main menu provides a list of sub-menus, each carrying out a particular group of functions; these sub-menus can be reached with a single key. Within these sub-menus, functions are carried out by using a two-letter code, so that, if you know the code for the function you want, you can specify it at the main menu level and so avoid the intervening step. Novice users, on the other hand, get the help of the menu approach, while the occasional user is helped by being able to see on a single screen, on request, all the two-letter commands available. Figure 33 shows the main *Tomorrow's Office* menu.

```
TOMORROW'S OFFICE    Thursday, 13th Jan. 1983    12:03:32    SoSoft

Functions                              Welcome to TOMORROW's OFFICE

1  Create Formats & Files              Enter the number beside the relevant
2  Insert & Maintain Records           option, then press RETURN.
3  Sort Records Into Order
4  Search File and Select Records      1–8 will produce a list of the
5  Create Print Formats & Print        programs related to the option chosen.
6  Automatic Update of Data File
7  File Management                      9 will produce a complete list of
8  System Management & User Menus       all the Tomorrow's Office programs.
9  Complete Menu On One Screen
0  Introduction to Menu                0 will cause the screen to re-
                                        appear as it is now.
f  Function Key Description
                                        At any time within this Menu program
en  End TOMORROW'S OFFICE              you can enter 0 to 9 for the options
                                        listed, or a 2-character program code.

Select Function [1 Char.] or Program [2 Chars.] or Introduction [0]
– <
TOMORROW'S OFFICE v    Current Data File Is              Vol.    On Disk
```

Figure 33 **Tomorrow's Office main menu**

Figure 34 shows the full list of *Tomorrow's Office* two-letter commands, as you would see it on request.

TOMORROW'S OFFICE		Thursday, 13th Jan. 1983		12:04:15 SoSoft	
Screen/Data Formats		Sorts		Jobs & User Menus	
Create Master Format	cm	Extract/Sort Index	es	Save Job	sj
Create Trans'n Format	ct	Re-Sort Index	rs	Run Job	rj
Amend Master Format	am	Re-Chain Transactions	rc	Create User Menu	cu
Amend Trans'n Format	at	Sort Transactions	st	Amend User Menu	au
Maths Input/Amend	ma	Re-Sort Trans'n Index	rt	Select User Menu	um
Screen Format Print	fp	Searches		File Updates	
Order of Input	oi	Select Search Criteria	sc	Select Update Criteria	uc
Alternate Format	af	Search File	sf	File Update	uf
Data Management		Simple Search	ss	Re-Calculate Maths	ur
Select Data File	sd	Reports & Labels		File & System Management	
Record Insert	ri	Create Print Format	pc	Create Data File	cr
Record Amend	ra	Maths Input/Amend	pm	Copy Data File	cd
Record Delete	rd	Print Compilation	pk	Delete Data File	dd
Record View	rv	Print Options	po	Control File Handler	fh
Batch Input	bi	Print File	pf	File/Volume Status	fs
Batch Update	bu	View/Print Records	vp	Convert & Copy	cc
Batch Delete	bd	Index View/Print	iv	File Output/WP Link	fo
Transaction Processor	tp	Create Label Format	lc	Change Peripherals	cp
External File Input	fi	Label Print	lf	Change Password	pw

Select Function [1 Char.] or Program [2 Chars.] or Introduction [0]
– <
TOMORROW'S OFFICE v   Current Data File Is   Vol.   On Disk

Figure 34 **Complete list of *Tomorrow's Office* options**

Where menus are used, consistency is particularly important. Similar options on different menus should be invoked in the same way. For instance, a good menu-driven system will always provide an 'escape route' from all levels of menu below the main menu entered when the package is run; this escape option should always be invoked using the same key.

Question-and-answer
As its title implies, this involves presenting a series of questions on the screen for the user to answer. One advantage is that a relatively detailed prompt can be given to explain the purpose of the question and the options available. Another is that the user is obliged to enter responses to items for which the system must have information. It can thus be a very useful method of getting responses to simple questions from novice users, especially if the system shows

clearly what default action will be taken if the question is bypassed. However, it can also take some time to elicit a set of responses in this way, and this becomes increasingly tedious as the user gains experience.

Form-filling

An alternative to question-and-answer is to use a form which the user 'fills in' by moving the cursor about on the screen. This approach has two major advantages. First, the user can see all the options, and is able to judge how they interact with one another. Second, since all the options are displayed with the default action, the user can alter only those responses which need changing, rather than answering 'No' or hitting the RETURN key in response to every question. However, these benefits are achieved at the expense of displaying less prompting information than is possible with the question-and-answer approach. Where lots of prompting is required, the latter approach would therefore be better, for example when the task is complex or the users inexperienced.

The method used by the package *Everyman* to find out what dimensions should be used to print a report shows an effective use of the form-filling technique. The package displays a diagram of a piece of paper, with the default values for each option shown. To change any of these, you just move the cursor to the particular value, and enter your own instead. The 'form' thus matches closely the medium about which information is being collected, and only a minimum of data need be entered. Figure 35 shows the various items which can be changed.

A neat touch is the single 'hole' pictured on the left of the page, which indicates that the report will be printed on single sheets of paper. By putting the cursor on this column and pressing the question-mark key, you can turn the single hole into a column of holes, to show that you have continuous paper in your printer.

Commands

In all the three approaches already discussed, the user is responding to requests for information from the system. The alternative is for the user to take the initiative, and issue a command to the system. This approach has several advantages, notably the ability to be

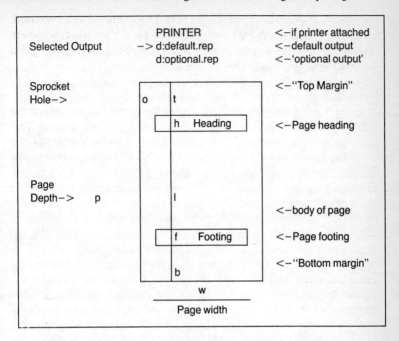

Figure 35 *Everyman* 'form' for specifying paper options

more flexible in giving instructions, to go straight to the part of the system in which action is required, and to invoke powerful features concisely. Figure 36 shows a *dBASEII* command to select a group of records and display one field from each of those selected, together with the output resulting from using the command with a small file.

.Display for 'pool'$Interests .and. (Title='Mrs' .or. Title='Miss') Surname

Albatross
Dragon
Eagle
Fox

Figure 36 **Concise dBASEII command for displaying part of
each selected record**

The disadvantages of commands are that the user must know what instructions are available, and be able to compose an instruction from scratch. The system can be quite helpful, however, in overcoming these disadvantages. Some systems display an abbreviated list of commands available at each point; when the user enters a command name, the system then indicates the format of the command and what may be included within it. This approach can do much to combine the benefits of commands with those of the methods more suited to novice users. An example of the display of *CardBox* command names is shown in Figure 37, and following it (Figure 38) the next level of options available once the SELECT command has been given.

```
CARDBOX(U)    File = B:CLUBMRS.FIL    PRINT
Level 0 – RECORD 3 OF 4
```

Member's number: Smith02	Title	Initials
Surname Smith		
Add1	Add2	
Add3	Postcode	
Date of joining	Membership grade	
Date last paymnt	Amount of paymnt	
Interests sailing, pool, tennis, table-tennis		

```
Enter command:
MAsk; SElect, INclude, EXclude; HIstory, BAck, CLear; LIstindex;
ADd, DUplicate, EDit, DElete; REad, WRite; FOrmat, PRint; SAve, QUit
LIST: ^R=1st ^C=last ^A=back ^F=fwd   ENTRY: ^X=erase ^H=backspace
```

Figure 37 **Commands displayed on the screen in *CardBox***

As we saw in the last chapter, the most powerful packages provide facilities which enable you to set up frequently needed sequences of operations. Most of these packages use commands, but some use mainly menus. This ability to customise your system can be very

```
CARDBOX(U)      File = B:CLUBMRS.FIL      PRINT
Level 1 – RECORD 1 OF 2
```

Member's number: Smith01   Title Mr   Initials A. B.
Surname Smith
Add1 14 Berry Road   Add 2 Parkway
Add3 SEASIDE   Postcode PL13 2HH
Date of joining 831213   Membership grade Family
Date last paymnt 831213   Amount of paymnt £20.00
Interests tennis, bowls, pool, table-tennis

```
Enter command: SELECT
Enter a field name followed by ''/'', or ''/'' only to specify all fields.
Fields are: MN TI IN SU A1 A2 A3 PC DJ MG DP AP IN
LIST: ˆR=1st ˆC=last ˆA=back ˆF=fwd   ENTRY: ˆX=erase ˆH=backspace
```

Figure 38 **Lists of options displayed after** *CardBox*
SELECT command issued

useful even for the user setting up the system for his or her own use.
It is invaluable for those setting up systems for others. The use of
stored instruction sequences makes it possible to exploit the power
of a complex package, while at the same time permitting its use by
novice users and by those who do not want or need to progress
beyond a limited knowledge of the package.

The ultimate in flexibility is provided by those packages which
allow access to the file handling facilities of the package from
programs written in conventional computing languages such as
Basic, Cobol or *C.* While such an approach has a considerable part
to play in the most extended uses of data management systems, its
detailed evaluation is beyond the scope of this book.

Documentation
Just as there is a variety of approaches to inviting instructions from
users, so there is a variety of types of documentation, and in each

case some are more suited to particular categories of user. It is common practice to provide a training guide or tutorial manual, which allows people to work their way through the facilities provided by the package before using it on 'real' data. The best training guides take you through the main aspects of the most important facilities in an orderly way, using examples supplied with the system. While doing so, they should relate the solution provided by the package to the kinds of problems met in practice. Such a guide should not, however, overwhelm novices with every last detail of esoteric facilities. A useful adjunct to the training guide (but rarely provided) is a 'cookbook' of typical problems and their solutions, such as 'how do I print labels?'

Once you are familiar with the system, you will want to be able to check more complex points quickly and easily. This is the function of the reference manual. Every manual should have an index, but the index to the reference manual is the most important of all. It should be of adequate size, should reference phrases as well as words, and should use terms meaningful to the user rather than the computing jargon which is common in the reference manual, even of those rare packages where the tutorial guide is clear and jargon-free.

For experienced users, especially those who use the package only occasionally, a reference summary (preferably pocket-sized and on lightweight card) is invaluable. It is also useful to users during training, giving them an oversight of all the facilities available in the package. The ability to see all the facilities listed on two sides of a single sheet of card or paper makes it much easier to get an overall picture of what the package can do and how it works.

The four major methods used to allow the user to give instructions to a package are all appropriate to different types of user and situation. A good compromise can be to use menus to reach the particular part of the system which the user needs, and then to use commands which are well prompted on the screen. If the image the system presents to the user is good enough, the documentation will become largely redundant. But even if this goal were to be achieved, documentation would still be important in training, for getting an overall picture of the package and its facilities, and for checking detailed points of reference.

19 Sharing information

In some circumstances, you may need to share information among several people, all of whom need to use it at the same time. Various degrees of sharing are possible; each will be discussed very briefly as they interact with the operation of a data management system. The general question of sharing a computer deserves detailed attention beyond the scope of this book.

In Chapter 17, we looked briefly at the problems of sharing information among several users of the same computer, where the computer may be used only by one person at a time. In some circumstances, your need for sharing may go beyond this, to enable several people to share information in such a way that they can all use the information at the same time.

The problems of sharing information to this extent can be substantial. First of all, you must have a computer which is physically capable of working in this way. Small business computers are in the main designed to be used individually. Furthermore, it rarely makes sense at present to share resources (except perhaps the use of a high-quality printer) purely as an economy measure; this is partly because the process of sharing uses for purely housekeeping purposes resources which could otherwise be at the disposal of the user.

If it is essential to share information, there are two ways in which physical sharing is possible. Either the whole computer is shared, with each user having just a screen and keyboard of their own, or else just the backing store is shared, with each user having processing power of his or her own. On small computers the first approach is liable to be slow, especially where a lot of keyboard entry and interrogation is taking place. The second approach is likely to give an acceptable speed of response to your requests.

In both cases, the data management package must be able to work with the operating system to provide the extra safeguards which are necessary when several users share the same backing store. The complexity of these safeguards depends on the extent of the sharing needed. If it is essential that everyone sharing the information has access to exactly the same information all the time, then users must be able to share data files.

For instance, in a company which takes telephone orders for its products using a computer to check the availability of stock, the check must always take place on the current state of the stock. Otherwise, you might say that an order can be filled from stock, only to find that your information is out of date and the goods are no longer in store. On the other hand, if several people can access information simultaneously, then there must be safeguards to make sure that the same item of stock cannot be reserved twice. This is usually achieved by allowing as many people as you like to view any record, but preventing more than one person being able to change it at a time. This process is usually called 'record locking', because the record is locked against change until the person with permission to change it finishes his or her task.

Some small business computers have the ability to support this activity, but few data management packages take advantage of these facilities. This is partly because the features which permit sharing tend to be highly specific to a particular make of computer. This situation is changing fast, but true shared access to files will always be more prone to difficulty than the independent use of files, because it is inherently a more complex process.

However, it is not always necessary to share information so completely. An alternative is to allow users to share backing store without allowing more than one person to access a file at the same time. In many circumstances this is enough; for instance, you can often arrange things so that information is split up into units which can be handled separately, and then merged later for processing. Many packages, though they do not have facilities for *record locking*, do have the ability to prevent a second user getting at a file which is already being used by someone else – that is, they provide a *file locking* feature.

A third possibility, which does not even require the users who wish to share to be connected to the same disk, is to exchange floppy disks. The separate computers must, of course, be able to read each others' disks, and this is not just a matter of being the same size – almost all computers use an idiosyncratic format of their own for writing floppy disks, and there are as yet few standards in this area. This approach does not require any special features to be available in the package, though there may be copyright restrictions on the use of the package on different computers. (Usually you will need to buy one copy for each computer, though some suppliers make special arrangements for several computers in the same office.)

Finally, you may be able to link separate computers by using communications lines. The implications for sharing information on a data management system depend on the approach, but they will be similar to the considerations involved in sharing a hard disk.

Sharing information is a matter of time and resources. If several users need immediate access to the same information, then you must be able to share files using record locking facilities. The availability of this feature will depend as much on your computer's operating system as on your data management package. The majority of packages are intended for one user at a time, and do not have record locking facilities, though quite a number can lock a complete file to prevent it being accessed by more than one person. This means that several people can share common information, provided any particular file is used only by one person at a time. But you may have to wait to get the information you need. The length of the wait depends on your application and on whether there is any way, through the computer or otherwise, to communicate with the person who is preventing your access. If you can afford to wait longer, it may be sufficient to exchange complete disks, in which case you need no special facilities in the package itself. This may be the only route open if you have or need to have separate computers (able to read the same disks), and cannot or do not wish to use networking facilities.

20 Sources of supply

*When you buy a package, you also buy any facilities the seller provides for training in the use of the package, and support and help in putting it to use. The **availability of support** may therefore influence you both in choice of package, and in choice of supplier.*

Buying a package

There are two main sources from which you can purchase a data management package: a computer dealer, or a mail-order distributor. A mail-order distributor is likely to be cheaper, and certain to have a much wider range of packages available. Indeed, for less commonly available packages on computers with unusual disk formats, mail-order may be the only source. However, you will not usually get any support or training as part of the purchase: you certainly will not get any training in the use of the package itself, although queries may be answered over the telephone. When learning about the package itself, you must rely on the documentation supplied with the package, or seek help from elsewhere. Mail-order distributors, and dealers who sell nationally through mail-order, advertise extensively in the popular computing magazines: for more details, see the section on Further Information at the end of this book.

Buying a package from a dealer – that is, a computer dealer close to your office – can be a hit-and-miss affair. If you already own a computer, you might expect to buy packages from the same source as the computer, but that may not be the best approach. A dealer should supply some training with the package, and should also be prepared to answer queries at least over the telephone. However, on small business computers the price of packages is low relative to the cost of selling them, so few dealers can afford to give more than the barest minimum of training, and some give none. The support staff employed by dealers are usually knowledgeable about only a proportion of the packages they sell. So it is well worth shopping around to find a dealer who has the necessary expertise and is prepared to provide at least some initial support.

In certain circumstances, you may not need any training from the supplier – perhaps you have friends or colleagues who can help you get to grips with the package. If this is the case, then it obviously makes sense to buy from the cheapest source. However, if you **will** need training and support, it is better to worry less about the small discounts which may be available, and look for a source of supply which offers some support. If you do, then it is important to get the commitment in writing, to avoid difficulties after you have paid for the package.

Packages are rarely guaranteed in the way that computers usually are. However, your statutory rights should be sufficient to protect you against serious malfunction, and any reputable firm, whether dealer or mail-order, should replace a copy of a package which cannot be installed. (I have personally never known such a thing happen to people whom I have advised. Packages are often hard to use, but they don't usually fail to work at all, at least on disk-based small business computers.)

Alternative sources of support

If you buy from a mail-order company or from a dealer who cannot give you any or enough support or training, there are other sources of help. Informal and often free sources include other users of the same package, and the user group if there is one. You may also get help from a local college or a specialist centre set up to help small businesses with computers. These sources may also provide more formal help for a fee, as may specialist firms who provide courses and advice on the major packages. Such firms often also offer a 'tailoring' service for more complex packages, to set them up in such a way as to meet your specific needs.

Where a package originates in your own country, or where there is a major importer or offshoot of the parent company, you may be able to obtain extra support from the manufacturer. Many manufacturers of data management packages hold regular training courses which are reasonably priced. Even more provide a 'hot-line' service, whereby users can telephone a central number for help with their queries. This may either be free to all registered users, or it may be available for a (usually small) subscription.

Data management systems may be bought from local computer dealers, or from mail-order firms. The quality and extent of the support they give varies from none to just enough to get started, though there are a few dealers who offer more help. A good source of further help and training, at a price, may be the manufacturer of the package. An alternative is to get help from a specialist training firm. Help in tailoring complex packages may also be available from companies who specialise in this work.

21 Planning and training

Once you have done all the hard work of analysing your require-ments and choosing a data management package to match, it may appear that all your preparations are over. However, if you next plan the implementation of your system carefully, you will reap rich dividends in the future in terms of a smooth beginning and trouble-free running. Planning should involve decisions about when to implement the system, what application is to be implemented, what preparation is required, and how to set the system up initially. In this chapter we look at the first two of these questions.

Timing and tasks

When we looked at the case study in Part 1, we saw that there was one particular application for which there was a pressing need for automation. Usually there is one major application which prompts you to implement a data management system, and you would expect to start with this application. However, this may not be appropriate. The first application you implement will involve you in learning a lot about your package, its quirks and clever points, and about the process of implementation. In so doing, you will make a lot of mistakes, and gain many new insights into the needs of your organisation when looked at in this light. If your 'priority' appli-cation is large and complex, especially if you are under pressure to get it right first time, you should probably choose to start with a smaller problem.

Another factor which should influence your decision about where to start and when is the schedules of the tasks which are candidates for automation. It is very dangerous to put in a new system at a time when the workload is heavy, and you or other users are under pressure. When the system is first installed, you must expect work to go **more slowly** for a while, while people get used to the new methods. Nor should you underestimate the work of entering preparatory information and of keeping the manual system going while you change over – more on this in the next chapter.

It is therefore sensible to start with a project which is not under heavy time constraints. If your priority project is large, complicated or always subject to tight deadlines, then start with something else and do your learning in less stressful and potentially disastrous circumstances. Finally, when choosing a slack time, make sure the slack is long enough. Remember Hofstadter's Law – applicable to most human plans but above all to those involving computers – which says that 'everything takes twice as long as you think it's going to, even when you've allowed for Hofstadter's Law. . .'.

Preparing to implement a data management system

The preparation phase should involve three kinds of activity: tasks which can be done before the package arrives, tasks such as training which need to be done after the package is installed but before it can be used in day-to-day work, and preparation of the data.

When you decided which package to buy, you should have discovered the whereabouts of the package users' group, if it exists. If you have not already done so, it is a good idea to join the group while you are still preparing to install your system, as members can often be of considerable help when you are getting off the ground.

At this stage, you should also make any necessary physical preparations. If you are installing a computer at the same time as your data management system, you will need to check such items as the siting of the system, ensuring that it will be in a reasonably clean environment free of static, that you avoid vibration by having a separate surface for the computer with its disk drives and for the printer, and so on. You will also need good and glare-free lighting around the computer, and desk space on which to put papers while working on the system.

Even if you already have the computer, two general points may become more important with the advent of a data management system. When your application involves a large amount of information, the system will be in use for long periods, perhaps for much

longer at a stretch. This will increase the likelihood of an interruption in the power supply or a surge caused by 'spikes'. ('Spikes'
usually happen when changes in loading occur, because there is
heavy equipment on the same power line – that is, the grid line
which supplies your office and probably several other offices or
factories. They may, however, be caused simply by having an
electric kettle on the same circuit.)

Computers vary a great deal in their tolerance of this kind of
interference, but in a bad case you could lose sizeable amounts of
information. Or, worse still, your data could be corrupted in a way
which you would find hard to detect, perhaps until some time
afterwards. It might then be impossible to repair the damage without a lengthy investigation, and substantial re-entry and re-
processing. (Unless your system takes a proper audit trail, which
you keep separately from the computer, such recovery may not be
possible at all.) If power supply problems are at all likely, it makes
sense to protect yourself against them. There are a number of
suitable and reasonably priced devices on the market, and your
computer dealer should be able to give you advice.

An existing computer will also already have a printer, but your
initial uses may not have involved extensive amounts of printing. If
you have large quantities of data to process, you are likely to
generate quite lengthy reports. Noise levels on the printer may then
become a problem. People are often surprised that the noise-levels
in a room containing several typewriters in constant use are bear-
able, but that the noise of a single printer operating continuously for
long periods is barely tolerable. The continuous operation is partly
responsible; in addition, the noise level on most 'daisy-wheel'
printers is higher than on a conventional typewriter.

Printer noise may be reduced by fitting an acoustic hood to the
printer. Alternatively, it may be better to have two printers: a
relatively quiet dot matrix printer which is used as much as possible,
and a daisy-wheel printer which is kept for situations where high
quality printing is essential. (The printing quality of dot-matrix is
usually quite acceptable for everything except letters and reports
which are sent outside the organisation.)

This solution can also help to ensure that your printers are sufficiently robust – many machines which double as typewriter and

printer cannot cope with heavy use. You should get a clear statement from the supplier about the rating of the printer, that is the
number of hours a day during which it should be capable of printing.
A simple dot matrix printer can cost no more than an acoustic hood,
and, when bought as a second printer, provides the additional
advantage of resilience (matrix printers tend also to be more
robust than daisy-wheel printers). Also, you will have two of the
devices which are the most vulnerable to malfunction.

Your dealer should have advised you about the need for a maintenance contract on your computer. If he has not, you should check
what your position is, and get it confirmed in writing. If your system
is essential to you, so that you could not do without it even for a day
or two, you should have a proper maintenance contract, with a
guarantee of 'call-out' time and of a replacement system if your own
cannot be repaired on the site. Such contracts are, however,
expensive. An adequate arrangement may be to pay for repairs if/as
they become necessary – though you will wait longer to get any
repairs done. A possible compromise is to have a maintenance
contract just for the printer, as it is the most likely piece of equipment to go wrong. (On the other hand, buying a second cheap
printer instead would probably save the cost of this maintenance in
less than a year.)

Effective guarantees and maintenance on software packages are
harder to come by (though of course your rights in law may protect
you in the case of really serious malfunction). Your best protection
is in numbers. If you buy a widely available package, thousands,
perhaps tens of thousands, of people are using it too, and, unless it is
a very new package, most of the *bugs* should have been ironed out.

At this preparatory stage, you should also check your supplies of
consumables. Now is the time to order any special stationery you
may need, and to make sure that you have a plentiful supply of disks
for taking security copies.

Training
In the discussion on sources of supply in Chapter 20, we saw that the
amount and nature of the training you get with the package will
depend on where you purchased it. We also saw that there are
alternative sources of training available, should you need more than

the seller will give. Here we look at the amount and nature of training you might need, and at the timing of this training in relation to the implementation of the system.

The package tutorial guide may be sufficiently clear for someone with an elementary understanding of computers, or even a complete novice who is enthusiastic and highly motivated, to learn about the package without outside help. If you plan to learn this way yourself, or if other people are to do so, it is very important to be orderly about the training process. You will come to grips with the package much more quickly and effectively if you take the time to work through the tutorial guide, doing the examples and exercises as you go.

If you have seen a really slick demonstration of a package by someone who knows the package really well, you may be lured into just dipping into the guide here and there, in the hope of finding out how to do particular things. For most people, this approach is a snare and a delusion. The guide is not designed to be used in this way, and most systems are sufficiently complex to repay putting some effort into learning about their facilities as such first, before trying to apply them in your environment.

Learning about a computer system is rather like learning to drive a car. You must come to terms with using the throttle, changing gear, steering, turning left or right, and then with the more complex manoeuvres like overtaking, before you are fit to drive on your own, let alone drive and navigate in a strange country at night and with ice on the roads. If you fail to take training in the use of the system seriously, you probably won't end up killing anyone. You will, however, waste a lot of your own and other people's time and effort, and may not achieve your objectives.

The scheduling of training is also very important. While it is vital to do some preparatory learning before applying the package to your own tasks, you should not explore the most abstruse features of a package before trying it out on your own data. Learning through examples in the manual is an important start, but it is only a start. When I train users, I do some initial training on the basics of the package itself (taking one or two complete days, according to the complexity of the package and the needs of the users' environment). I then leave the users to practise for a while, using examples which reinforce the learning about the package itself and simple tasks to help put that learning into practice within the organisation concerned. After a short time, a few days or perhaps a week, another day's training takes place. During this day we discuss all the problems which have come up in practice, and explore some of the more complex features of the package.

Once training is complete, your main source of day-to-day information about the package will be the documentation. However, you will rarely have another chance to take a reasonably leisured look at the package. Unless you become reasonably familiar during training with all the documentation you may need, you will not find it easy to extract information from the manuals in a hurry. So it makes a lot of sense to try and get used to the manuals during the training period. This applies especially to the reference manual if you need to use the full facilities of the package. This is made much easier if the tutorial guide, and the 'help' which the system gives you on the screen, refer by section or page number to the reference manual.

Planning the procedures needed

Your own application of a data management system will be unique, and will involve a knowledge of your tasks as well as of the data management system itself. It is therefore equally important for people to know how to use your particular implementation. (Where the package has been extensively tailored, this knowledge is probably more important than a detailed understanding of the data management system.) This material should be taught as part of the training, and it should also be documented carefully. Even if you are always going to operate the system yourself, many errors will be prevented by writing down your method of working. This is especially true of the procedures needed to carry out security copying, which will protect you and your valuable information from human mistakes and computer and package malfunction. More will be said about such procedures in the section on day-to-day running in the next chapter.

In this chapter, we have looked at the main points to be considered in implementing a working data management system. You should begin with your most important application, provided it is not too large or too complex, and provided that you install the system when staff are not under heavy pressure of work. In preparation for setting up the system, you need to make sure that those who will operate it are given proper training.

22 Setting up the system

Once the planning has been done, and training begun, you are ready to begin setting up your system. At this stage, important tasks include testing out your plans with some kind of dummy run and transferring existing information on to the new system. You will be wise to continue running your manual system in parallel with the new system for a while, to make sure all the problems have been ironed out.

Testing out your plans

An application which is complex, or which must work very well from the beginning, needs to be tested out very carefully. It can be very useful to carry out a 'pilot' experiment, using a small amount of data, but simulating the real situation, and using the procedures you have set up. A pilot can give you invaluable practical experience, and allow you to make necessary modifications before large amounts of information have been entered into the system. This is particularly true where you cannot change the structure of your records once they contain information, or where this is a tedious and time-consuming process.

Entering existing records

If you are transfering from an existing manual system, you will probably have to transfer records from index cards or paper files to the computer-based system. It is important not to underestimate the time needed to enter these records. You should remember that the people who are entering them will, at the same time, be getting used to the data management system and perhaps to the computer itself. (Even the keyboard may be rather different from those on typewriters). However, you may be able to turn this requirement to advantage, since entering this material can help people to get practice before starting on the 'live' data.

If you have large amounts of historical information to enter, it may be worth employing temporary staff for the purpose, or putting the work out to an agency which uses the same system. The big difficulty is that information does not stand still. For instance, in our club membership example, entering members' names and addresses may not change too often, but the current financial status of a proportion of the membership may change quite frequently. It may be necessary to separate the historical information which is not likely to change much from that which changes rapidly. The volatile information can then be entered last, just before the system goes into active use – preferably when your office is closed.

Changing over to an automated system

Once any initial or historical information has been entered, you are ready to transfer at least some work to the new system. However, you should normally continue to run your manual system side-by-side with the computer system for some time after the computer system appears to be running successfully. This is important even if you have carried out a careful pilot study and are as sure as you can be that everything will go smoothly. If your business would go bankrupt if the information on the computer system were completely lost, then you should continue running the manual system in parallel for at least three months. You should also make sure that you always keep some paper records, from which you could make at least a partial recovery if there were a serious problem. For information which is not so vital, you can probably stop using the manual system earlier.

Parallel running is not a popular approach, since everyone tends to feel they are under enough pressure from using a new system, without having to double the load by continuing to do the work by hand in the old way. But it can prevent very serious problems if some unforeseen eventuality arises, or if something goes wrong – which is very likely to happen in any new situation.

Day-to-day running

To run the system in an orderly way, you need some written procedures. These are especially important in two areas: input and updating information, and taking of security copies. The extent to which you need to document these functions will, of course, depend on how closely the system is tailored to your needs. For instance, if the system allows you to construct menus of your own, you can avoid the necessity of knowing and specifying file names. You may also be able to ensure that updating takes place in the correct sequence. For instance, in the club example you may need to send out reminder letters to people planning to take holidays who have not yet made their final payment. You also have changes to make because some members have moved house. The address changes should clearly be made first, in case they affect the destinations of the reminder notes. Nevertheless, this kind of detail is often missed unless a regular procedure is written down and followed.

This need for regular, written procedures is even more important where security copying is concerned. For this purpose, you should have several separate disks to use in rotation. This ensures that, even if a failure occurs while copying, you cannot lose more information than the amount entered since the time you last took a security copy. One possible approach is to have a set of five data disks, one for each day of the week, and to copy the most recent set of information on to the oldest disk at the start or end of each day's work. You would also be wise to take some precautions against fire, perhaps by taking one day's disk home and leaving it there until it is needed again on the corresponding day in the following week. Everyone thinks such disaster can never happen to them, but they can and do.

In this chapter, we have looked at the final stage of setting up a data management system. This stage will include ensuring that any existing information needed to operate the system correctly is entered into the data management system. While you are changing over to the new method, you should continue to operate the existing system in parallel for a time. Once the system is installed, it is much more likely to run smoothly if you follow regular procedures for updating records and for taking security copies of your information.

Part 4
Data management systems in practice

Throughout this book, we have seen many examples of the ways data management systems provide particular functions. In the last part, we look at the application described in our case study as a complete project, and follow through the stages of analysis described in the body of the book. In this part, we shall integrate this material to make a choice of package; instances of real packages are used to illustrate the various aspects. Remember that these instances have been chosen to make particular points; no comment is intended on the general merits of the packages mentioned, nor is the coverage in any way complete. (Several excellent packages have not been mentioned.) If you want more help in choosing between the packages available for your application, consult the appendix on sources of further information.

23 Practical implementation of a straight-forward problem

In this chapter, we look at the various stages you might need to go through if you were implementing the club membership system we have used in many of our detailed examples. No new ideas are introduced: rather, the material in the earlier parts of the book is used to guide you through the practical problems of analysing and planning the implementation of a relatively straightforward application.

From the description of the case study in Chapter 2, it is clear that the club feels its priority need to be a system to process members' subscriptions. This is relatively straightforward, though other applications which may be implemented later are more complex. Club membership is therefore a good place to start. It will also pay to implement it in a simple way, to learn how the system works, rather than trying to be too clever to begin with. For this reason, the club has not ruled out the possibility of choosing a very simple package to start with, which, though it cannot be expanded to meet other needs, provides a good vehicle for getting people used to the whole idea of computerisation.

Tasks the system must be able to perform
The basis for the club membership system is the card used in the manual card index already in use, together with the needs for processing the membership subscription information identified by the secretary and chairman. The club's needs are:

- to send letters to members whose subscriptions are due;
- to send reminders to those whose subscriptions are overdue;
- to find out easily at any time the current state of the club's subscription income;

- to locate members with particular interests;
- to be able later to process the holiday booking records.

Information which the system should store

To do all these tasks, the system must store several items of information. In the manual system, the record card stores the name and address, the date the member joined, his or her annual subscription and interests, and the years for which the subscription has been paid. As a reminder of the format, an example is shown below.

Seaside Sports and Social Club

Family member

Mr A. B. Smith
14 Berry Road
Parkway
SEASIDE
PL13 2HH

Joined: 13 December 1983
Annual subscription: £20.00
Years paid: 1983

Interests: tennis, bowls, pool, table-tennis

Figure 39 **Card from manual card index system**

Clearly, the computerised record should contain name and address, in order to be able to send out letters. However, since the club secretary, Ken, would like to be able to send 'personalised' letters to everyone, it will be necessary to store the name as three separate items: title, initials, surname. The whole set of three can then be used on the address label, while in the salutation of the reminder letter only title and surname will be used, to get a line of the form 'Dear Mr Smith'.

The date the member joined must be stored to calculate entitlement to life membership. This can then be used to determine when to send out reminder letters. To keep proper records of who has paid their subscription and who has not, the date – perhaps only the year – of the most recent payment must be stored. Finally, the subscription due from the member must be available for inclusion in the reminder letter. At first, Ken thought he would record the subscription due, just as he does in the manual card index. However, subscriptions change quite often. So he decided to ensure that the data management package chosen could store a table of values, which could be 'looked up' by a reporting program before printing letters. Such a table would contain a single set of subscription rates. Ken could then store just the membership grade in the member's record. (The grade will change less often, and only for individual members rather than for all.) If subscription rates change, he then need change only that one table, not every member's record.

The need to store information about members' interests poses a different problem: the information is essentially variable in quantity, and furthermore Ken will need to get at individual interests without knowing the order in which they were entered. Ideally, he would like a package which allows him to search for a particular interest anywhere within a field, and which uses only the amount of space necessary for interests actually recorded. The latter criterion is less important, as there are not too many types of interest which could be entered. If the package can look up abbreviated codes in a table, there may be very little wasted space.

The final choice Ken has to make concerns the way records will be identified when recalled for editing – say when a member pays his or her subscription. As we saw in Chapter 4, there are many advantages to using surnames, but that can give rise to inaccuracy and ambiguity. So Ken decided to use a code of the type we have already discussed, formed from the first five letters of the surname together with a two-digit code to distinguish the different families of Smiths, Joneses and Pengellys. For the convenience of those who do not like codes, Ken decided also to permit retrieval of the record directly through the surname. A possible format for the subscription record, given this specification, is shown overleaf.

Communication needs
The membership system will, to start with, be self-contained, but the need may arise to copy the information into a 'transport format'.

```
┌─────────────────────────────────────────────────────────────┐
│                                                               │
│                 Club Membership Record System                 │
│                                                               │
│   Member's number_____1   Title_____2   Initials_____3 │
│                                                               │
│   Surname_____4   │
│                                                               │
│   Add1_____5   Add2_____6         │
│                                                               │
│   Add3_____7   Postcode_____8           │
│                                                               │
│   Date of joining_____9   Membership grade_____10 │
│                                                               │
│   Date of last subscription payment_____11   Amount of payment £____12 │
│                                                               │
│   Interests_____13  │
│                                                               │
└─────────────────────────────────────────────────────────────┘
```

Figure 40 **Sample format for subscription record**

When the system is first set up, the structure of the records is bound
to be experimental, and Ken may later decide that he needs to store
more items of information. Many packages allow you to change the
structure of records only by copying them to a transport format and
back into the package format. Also, if the club decides to go for a
simple system which could not cope with the holiday bookings
application, it may subsequently be necessary to transfer all the
membership information to another package.

How much information?
At the moment, the club has around 600 members, of whom some
are 'family' members, so there are about 400 subscription payments
each year. The record shown above would take up about 250
characters, so the total amount of information would be about
100,000 characters. The package will need space to construct
indexes for key fields, and some space may also be needed for
sorting; nevertheless, this size of file can be comfortably accom-
modated on typical small business computers, which usually have
room for at least 300,000 characters on each disk drive.

Speed of retrieval is not likely to be a major problem either. For direct retrieval through an index, the number of records in the file should not make much difference to speed. With only 400 records, even searches (such as the issue of subscription reminders) which could involve checking every record should not take too long in most packages. However, this was a point Ken decided to check carefully.

The printing of reminder letters each month is likely to be the most time-consuming activity. With 400 members, renewals will take place at the rate of about 35 a month. About a third of the membership do not pay first time, and some need two reminders, so about 50 letters will be sent out at a time. Even without automatic sheet feeding, this should not take more than a couple of hours, so the club typist, Margaret, who works two hours each morning, should be able to do the work within a morning session.

Maintenance

For this application, Ken decided that one screen format would suffice, since the amount of information is neither large nor, in practice, very confidential. (Margaret sees all the manual records at the moment, and therefore knows which members are very overdue with their subscriptions. If she were less discreet, Ken's decision might have been different.) If possible, the total amount of subscription paid this year so far, and the amount of arrears outstanding, will be kept as running totals. Otherwise, Ken will set up a standard report, so that Margaret can get the information out whenever the chairman needs it.

Using the system

To begin with, Ken will set up the format of the records and of the reports needed, and Margaret will do the actual entry, maintenance and retrieval of the information. Later, as they become more accustomed to the system, they will both be able to make *ad hoc* use of the system. Neither has any experience of computers, so the system the club chooses will have to be very simple to operate, and forgiving of mistakes, without being tediously prolix.

At present, it will be easy to do the work of maintaining the club membership with a single system – indeed, it will have plenty of spare capacity – so the problem of sharing does not arise. Were it to do so, the club would need to take professional advice, since in the current state of the art this area can be very difficult for people without much experience of computing.

Sources of supply

One of the club members is a computer dealer, and has promised to give the club a favourable deal when it buys the computer system. The club committee appreciate the value of this offer, and of the fact that they are likely to get good maintenance service from this dealer. However, they know they will not get independent advice from him, and it is very important for relationships within the club that there is no hassle about the purchase. So they decided to ask a couple of people who have already bought computers from him how they have fared, in order to get a 'second opinion'. The result was favourable as far as the computer itself was concerned, but the users Ken spoke to had not been very impressed with the training he gave. Ken had in any case been rather wary about asking the dealer to do the training, as he does not get on very well with Margaret. So the committee decided to buy their system from the member, but to go elsewhere for training, even though that meant paying extra.

Implementing the system

The next question to decide was the best time to begin running the new system. After some thought, Ken decided that the best time would be in the early summer. At that time, fewer local members apply to join the club as they are busy preparing for the summer holiday season, but the visitors have not yet started to arrive in large numbers, so the load on the office is lower than usual. At this point, Ken realised that he had not given any thought to the question of recording temporary members' details, or including their payments in the accounts. The latter could be a serious omission, since summer visitors taking out temporary membership, are a substantial source of club income. He decided that the best thing to do would be to continue the manual system for temporary members for the time being – this had always been recorded properly as the retiring secretary didn't have time to get to know them – and then incorporate them into the computer system later. There did not seem to be any additional problems associated with recording information about temporary members.

The next question to settle was when and how to enter the existing records. Since the volume of records is not very great, Ken reckoned it would take about 14 hours – two minutes per record – to type them in. He calculated that if Margaret were to spend about an hour each day on the task, entry of the records could be completed within a month. It would therefore be possible to 'freeze' the system during this time. Thus the only major problem that remained was how to move from one subscription renewal date each year, to 12 renewal dates according to the month in which the member originally joined. The committee looked at several possibilities, including giving members a 'holiday' from payment from the end of the calendar year until the month in which the subscription would become due. That seemed likely to have too serious an effect on club income, so in the end it was decided to ask every member to pay an interim subscription spanning the period from January to the new month of subscription renewal.

In order to make it easy to enter information about new members to the system, Ken decided to have some forms printed which could be filled in when people join. These forms will be used by Margaret to add new members to the computer; this will be her first task each morning, together with updating the records of members who have paid their subscriptions. On the last working day of each month, Margaret will run off the reminder and 'defaulters' letters. To make sure that the change to the new system will go smoothly, Margaret will also continue to keep the manual card index up to date for the first three months.

In this chapter, we have looked at the various aspects of choosing and implementing a data management system for the club membership records. In the next chapter, we shall apply the results of the analysis to the choice of a particular package, and note the factors involved. In order to make the discussion clearer, we have talked as though it were possible completely to separate analysis from package choice, but you will realise that, in practice, these two processes would interact.

24 Choosing a package for the membership record system

In real life, at this point you would actually have to choose a package, after going through the pros and cons of the possibilities. Here, the aim is to illustrate the process of assembling those arguments, rather than to make a choice which would apply to a very specific situation. So in this chapter we look at the arguments in a way which should help you to go through the same process using your own criteria.

A major aim in the first stage of the club system is to keep it simple. Ken and his friends are therefore very tempted to choose a package which, though it has limited facilities, is very easy to use. *CardBox* is an example of such a package. The need to retrieve individual interests would be well catered for, and the requirement for finding records of members whose subscriptions were due could be met, although not very prettily. *CardBox* does not have an explicit date format. Ken would therefore have to store the month of renewal in a field and ask if it were equal to the current month, or else store the date of joining as DD/MM/YY and, for instance, search for the set of characters/12/ to find subscriptions due in December. However, *CardBox* cannot do arithmetic, so it would not be possible to find out the current state of subscription payments overall. Nor could you use a table to relate subscription and membership grade. Since *CardBox* does not allow you to link two data files, it would also be necessary either to treat the holiday bookings application separately when the time came, or move the data to another package which could provide such a link.

Another simple system, with a cost comparable to that of *Card-Box*, is *Friday!* It uses much the same approach to data organisation as *dBASEII* (it is produced by the same company), but is easier to use. *Friday!* can do arithmetic, and it has a table facility plus good features for formatting standard letters and labels. Although it does not have a special date format, *Friday!* can handle dates quite conveniently. It uses the same very flexible approach to handling parts of character formats that we saw in some of the examples of *dBASEII* commands; this would provide an appropriate method of handling the interests field. However, *Friday!* fields are limited to 32 characters, so you would have to use the table function in combination with the interests field, or split interests over two fields, to accommodate records about people with many interests. Apart from this not very significant drawback, *Friday!* would be quite appropriate for this application. However, this package does not have any facilities for linking files together. For this feature, you would need to move to its 'elder brother', *dBASEII*, a process which is completely straightforward in terms of data transfer but not necessarily so in terms of ease of use.

Facilities for linking files together are provided by *Pearl*, another package in the same 'budget' price level as the first two mentioned. *Pearl* can do arithmetic, and provides a table facility through its ability to display information from several files at once. It has flexible reporting features, and could provide the main facilities necessary to link the holiday and subscription records. The only area in which it would have significant drawbacks is in the processing of the 'interests' field. In common with many other packages in this price bracket, you cannot search within a field for a particular set of characters, so it would not be practicable to store all 'interests' in one field. The alternative would be to store each interest in a separate field. However, you would then need to be able to apply the same test to several fields, and ask for every record which passed any one of the tests. Unfortunately *Pearl* does not have this feature; if you wish to apply more than one test, then the record is selected only if all the tests are passed.

So much for examples of 'budget' range packages. Among the more expensive packages, there are many which would cope easily with this problem. Ken decided to look at three, which seemed to have considerable potential for use in the holiday booking application too. The first, *Delta*, uses a transaction processing approach, but used simply to store subscriptions as a set of master records it could provide all the features required.

dBASEII could also, apart from the same awkwardness with dates as *Friday!*, provide all the necessary facilities, with greater flexibility in the way files can be linked; but many people find it difficult to use, and it undoubtedly takes longer to learn than some menu-driven packages.

A third possibility is *BusiFile*, which is primarily menu-driven, but which uses some other techniques as well, to make it easier to drive the package quickly when you become able to take advantage of the short-cuts. Ken thought it had all the facilities he needed for the membership subscription system, and seemed reasonably easy to use. However, when he first looked at the package, he could not tell whether the features for linking files would be adequate for the holiday bookings project, as they were still under test. So another possibility was to reserve judgement about these features, and while waiting to see how they would turn out, to implement the membership system using the basic features.

It was becoming clear to Ken that, while there were many possible solutions to the membership records problem, there were far fewer options open if membership records were to be linked with holiday booking records. The committee decided to look more closely at that problem before making up its mind – and so shall we.

Many packages can cope well with processing simple types of record which closely mirror a manual card index, in which the information has a regular structure. Good facilities for handling lists, like the 'interests' field in our example, are less common. If your requirements include processing information which has a more complex structure than that provided by the card index model, the options are fewer and also more complex. In the next chapter, we look at the requirements of such an application.

25 Processing holiday bookings

This chapter follows the same procedure as that used in Chapter 23, this time for the holiday bookings project. The aim is to identify the main factors which should determine the choice of package for this project, and to highlight areas of potential difficulty in co-ordinating the collection of information with its storage and processing on the computer.

Tasks the system must be able to perform

The manual system for recording holiday bookings for club trips uses a card index, with each booking recorded on a single card. This will form the basis of the record in the computer system. Processing requirements include tasks carried out – sometimes with difficulty – at the moment, and also tasks of which the present system is incapable. The holidays organiser, Donald, wants the system to:

- produce reminder letters for those who have not yet paid the full cost of their holiday (reminder letters are sent out two months before departure date, as full payment is due six weeks in advance);
- print a pick-up list, in order of the pick-up points, and with total numbers of passengers in each of the three categories adults, children and senior citizens;
- send out joining instructions for each group of travellers;
- produce figures showing total revenue to date, and total sum still owing;
- prevent the entering of further bookings once a holiday is full;
- issue a warning if a holiday is nearing the last date for cancellation, and does not have enough bookings to break even.

Information which the system should store

To be able to send out reminders about payment, joining instructions and so on, the system must have access to the names and addresses of travellers. It must store booking information, including the numbers booked in each of three groups, adults, children and senior citizens, and the point at which the party is to be picked up. There must be a record of the total cost of each booking, and of the amount paid so far. An example of the card which is used to hold this information in the manual system is shown below. This card does not, however, contain any information about the holiday as a whole other than the departure date. The computer system will need this information to give warning of holidays being over- or under-booked.

```
                 Seaside Sports and Social Club
                        Holiday Trips

Holiday: Bondi Beach                              Mr A. B. Smith
Number in party: 3 adults                         14 Berry Road
                 2 children                       Parkway
                 2 senior citizens                SEASIDE
Date of departure: January 14 1984                PL13 2HH

Total cost of holiday: £3215.50
Deposit paid: £1100
Amount to pay: £2115.50

Pick-up point: Promenade
```

Figure 41 **Card from manual card index of holiday bookings**

The information about name and address will also appear in the member's subscription record, and would ideally be extracted from it for reporting purposes. The information about the total cost of the holiday depends on two factors: the numbers in the party of each category of traveller, and cost of each category. The information about cost will, of course, be the same for every party (with one exception – see below). It would therefore be better if this information, and other details such as departure date, could be stored just once. The total cost of the holiday should be calculated by the system from the factors shown. However, it does need to be calculated **and stored**, because there is one circumstance in which the prices may change but the costs to people already booked should not. If a holiday is selling slowly, but has passed its cancellation date, Donald will sometimes, with the committee's agreement, reduce the price for people making last-minute bookings. But of course this reduction would not apply to people who have already booked!

The system must also store the amount of money still owing on the holiday; this figure can be calculated in one of two ways. When a payment is made, the sum can be entered on the booking record, and the package can then calculate the amount still owing. The disadvantage with this approach is that the club has a record only of the most recent payment made by the traveller. If there is any query about previous payments, Donald will have no means of checking the details. A better alternative might be to record payments separately from the booking record, and to update the accumulated items on the booking record from those payment records. This approach recognises that, in fact, each booking is likely to involve several payments – another one-to-many relationship, like the one-to-many relationship between holiday and bookings.

To show the total revenue and amount owing for a holiday, Donald could simply request a report each time. If the information about a whole holiday trip is stored only once, then it is a simple matter to include a field to receive these totals in the same record. This can then be displayed whenever it is needed, without having to process each record and produce a report.

Ideally, then, each booking record should contain just the minimum information necessary to identify and process that individual record. The information which is shared with the member's subscription record should be accessed for display and reporting purposes only. Likewise, the information which applies to every booking for one holiday should be stored separately from the booking records, so that the information is not duplicated. This approach would minimise Donald's problems in keeping the information accurate and up-to-date.

FORM LAYOUT (PAGE 1) FOR HOLIDAY

Club Membership Record System

Member's number______1 Title______2 Initials______3
Surname______4
Add1______5 Add2______6
Add3______7 Postcode______8

Number in party: Adults______9 Children______10 OAPs______11
Pickup point______12

Amount of this payment______13

Total cost of holiday______14 Amount paid______15 Amount to pay______16

Holiday______17 Departure date______18
Maximum number____19 Adult cost____20 Child cost____21 OAP cost____22

Figure 42 **Possible display format for holiday booking record**

The record shown above gives an example of how this might be achieved. The information at the top, above the first heavy line, comes from the member's subscription record, while the information below the second heavy line comes from a file containing a single record about each holiday the club is running.

Communication needs

It is likely that Donald will need to experiment quite a bit with the structure and processing of this project, as it is much more complex than the basic membership subscription system. So he will need to be able to make changes, either within the package or by copying to an external format and reading back. The only other situation in which the need for communication might arise is as an alternative way of providing a link to the membership records. More about this in the next chapter.

How much information?

If it is possible to store each item of information only once, then the storage requirements of this application are very small. Each booking record would need to contain only about 50 characters of data, so with perhaps 200 bookings stored at any one time, the records would occupy only 10,000 characters. This assumes that the booking record is updated 'on the fly' each time a payment is made; if a record is kept of each payment, then slightly more space would be needed.

Maintenance

It will be much easier to ensure that the booking records are up to date if the fields are calculated or derived from elsewhere where appropriate, along the lines we discussed when deciding what information the club would need to store. It will also help in this if the system can check, when a booking is entered, whether or not a holiday is fully booked. It may be harder to trigger automatically the check on possible underbooking. Donald may be able to specify that an action is carried out once each time the package starts to process a set of records; if so, then he would be able to ask the package to check for underbooking every time new bookings are taken or payments made. If a holiday is going slowly, however, there may not be much activity of this kind. Another possibility is for the system to run various date-dependent procedures automatically, at the start of every day. The total number booked would then be checked if the last cancellation date were, say, two weeks away or less, and any underbooking would be reported. Such an approach works best if summary information is stored rather than having to be aggregated by reading every record – you would not want to be kept waiting to start a day's session while the system read every record in a large set.

The record shown in the example above now displays quite a lot of information on the screen; Donald and Margaret may not want to have all this information shown all the time. Most screen amendment will involve recording payments and checking summary information on revenue and booking numbers. The address and pick-up information will probably be used only for printing. The date of departure is recorded mainly for the system to use in producing reminder letters and other circulars whose timing is related to that date. So another helpful feature would be the ability to define 'windows' on to the records, making it possible to display just parts of the record.

An alternative approach is to regard each section of information – data from the subscription record, from the holiday record, from the booking record and perhaps also from a separate set of payment records – as distinct, for display purposes. It would then be necessary to decide what information from other parts of the record system should be displayed, for instance with the payment record when entering a holiday payment. This approach corresponds to that used by *Everyman*, with its ability to have several 'layers' of data according to the structure of the information. An example of how a structure for processing the whole club project might look is shown in the next chapter, where we shall look more closely at this kind of approach.

Using the system

The system will be used in much the same way as for the membership records, with Margaret doing most of the day-to-day work, and Donald setting the system up and carrying out *ad hoc* reports. However, one of the problems with the manual system was a lack of co-ordination between people taking bookings, and if this were to persist on the computer system it could become unworkable. So Donald has decided to recruit another club member, Iris, expressly to co-ordinate all bookings, and make sure they are entered into the computer regularly. The considerations on supply and training are very similar to those on the subscription system, and the solutions will therefore also be the same.

Changing over to the new system presents few problems. As each new holiday is set up, it will be put on to the computer, although manual records will be maintained in parallel for a while, as Donald cannot face the thought of all those irate holidaymakers if any information were to go astray.

Booking records will be updated twice a week, and a weekly check made to see if any reminders are due, in which case an appropriate set of letters will be printed. The same process will be used to check for underbooking, unless the package chosen is able to do that without being prompted.

The requirements for day-to-day running of the holiday booking system are straightforward, and training and implementation should present no special problems once an appropriate package has been chosen to match the more complex structure of the data. That choice is the subject of the next chapter.

26 Choosing a package for the holiday booking system

So far, we have looked at the factors which would directly influence the choice of a package for the holiday booking project. But this choice is also influenced by the needs of the club as a whole, both in linking the membership records to those for holiday booking, and in setting up a structure which might be appropriate to the needs of other club records, such as stock items, when that project comes to fruition.

In the last chapter, we used a record format created in *Pearl* as an example of the way the holiday records might be set up. This would have given Donald most of the features he wanted, using running totals rather than keeping details of separate payments. However, it would be interesting to see if other solutions might enable Donald to keep a separate record of each payment made, so that they could be checked if any queries arose.

Another solution we looked at in Chapter 5 was the use of a transaction-based package (our example was based on *Delta*). You remember that these packages keep a master record together with one or more sets of transaction records associated with each master. This assumes a two-level hierarchy of information. Such an approach would deal quite adequately with the holiday booking records, including keeping a separate record of each payment, were this system to be independent of the subscription records. (Indeed, an example of such a system is included in the *Delta* manual). However, there is no easy way to mirror a three-tier structure using a master transaction approach. So it would not be possible for both the subscription record and the holiday master record to feed information into the bookings record in the way the club would like.

An alternative option we looked at in Chapter 5 was to use *dBASEII*. This does not restrict the structure of relationships between sets of records, but does not, on the other hand, make any very special provisions for records with a complex structure. Since you can have only two files available at any one time, it would be necessary to retrieve information from the subscription record file and the holiday master record file in turn, closing each file after each access. The processing requirements of holiday booking, such as detecting when a holiday is full, could also be accomplished, by tailoring the package using the *dBASEII* command language. So the basic approach of separating holiday payments, bookings, master holiday information and subscription records would be possible, but with some effort on the part of Donald and his friends.

Another possibility is to use a package such as *Everyman*, which expressly allows for complex structures. A possible approach to storing our four sets of records was given in Chapter 5, with holiday payments feeding information to a booking record, which in turn would update the holiday master record. The structure diagram is repeated below, because it provides a clear picture of one approach to describing the structure in question. This is not to say that this would necessarily be the right choice in this particular situation, rather that the diagram mirrors well the actual structure of the real-life data.

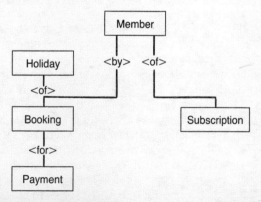

Figure 43 **A possible structure for the club project**

I said at the beginning of Chapter 23 that the important point here was not to choose a particular package, but to see how such a choice could be arrived at. In real life, Donald and Ken and the committee would go on to take up some of the further sources of information suggested in the appendix, in particular talking to other users with similar problems, and then decide. My hope is that in following their problems and potential solutions through the course of this book, you have been encouraged to analyse your own application in a similar way, and that you will find the approach and its practical application successful. In the last chapter and the Appendix we try to cross a little further over that gap between applications and the solutions which data management systems can provide. The next chapter suggests the considerations which lead to the choice of a data management system rather than other types of package. The Appendix provides a set of checklists for those who want detailed pointers to choosing a specific data management package.

27 Choosing a package for your system

*You should now be in a position to decide on the needs for your own system. In this chapter you will find some guidance on when these might be met by a **specialist package**, when a **data management system** may do the job, and when you may need to write or commission a **specially written program**. Where a data management system is needed, you will need to consider how it will relate to other applications, and whether an **integrated package** which includes data management features might be appropriate.*

Every business, every practice, every department is different. So to some extent at least every computer application is also different from every other, and as a result a book cannot tell you exactly how to apply computers in your business. The aim of this chapter is to take you a little further across that gap between your objectives and the implementation of those objectives on a computer.

Special package, data management system, program?
After reading this book, you may still feel that what you want to do is so unusual that you must have a program specially written for your requirements. If you choose this route, then either you will need to spend a great deal of money – if the software is for a microcomputer, probably two or three times the cost of the computer system itself – or else you will have to expend a lot of your own effort and time in learning how to program, and then writing the program yourself. Sometimes this route is the only possible way of achieving your goals, but you should be very wary of coming to this conclusion. A compromise may well be to choose an appropriate data management system, and commission the supplier, or a

specialist in tailoring the package, to set up the initial system for you. This approach is likely to be much cheaper, less error-prone, faster to complete, and more flexible, than writing or commissioning a program suite written in a computer language such as Basic.

At the other end of the spectrum from specially-written programs or tailored systems are the packages marketed for a specific task: suites Hotel Bookings, Printers' Job Costing, Television Rental, Crop Rotation. Some of these packages provide quite powerful facilities for a particular set of tasks. Since they are aimed at your specific application, they should be less work to implement than a more general-purpose system. Often, however, you pay a price in lack of flexibility; it may not be possible to adapt the package to allow for the unusual individual features found in every business or group. In addition, for many applications there is no appropriate package. In such circumstances, if you have a small business, it is often tempting to begin by buying an accounting package, and to start by automating your accounts. Accounts packages tend to be slightly more general in their use than packages written for specific applications such as conference management. Most businesses do have purchase, sales and nominal ledgers, and do conform to standard accounting practices if only at the behest of their auditors. But it is common to find that, having set up a complete accounting system including all your customers' names and addresses, you cannot then get at those names and addresses except as the package dictates. So you cannot, for instance, make use of the information you have already stored in order to send all your customers a letter about this month's special offer.

It is possible that you may be quite sure that your requirements are firm, and that an applications package or an accounting package has all the facilities you will need. Or you may feel that a particular package comes sufficiently close to providing an appropriate solution to make it preferable to a more general-purpose approach. A third possibility is to start with an adequate special package, and to transfer later to something more general when you have some experience. In all these circumstances, you will improve your chances of success if you bear in mind the points shown in this list:

Is the package based on a data management system, or written in a programming language? Several of the most powerful data management systems have been used as a basis for special packages and accounting suites, as an alternative to programming them in Basic or another computer language. This approach can provide much greater flexibility at little extra cost.

Can the package write all the records out to a standard 'ASCII text file'? If this is possible, you should be able to move up to a more powerful package later if necessary. If it can't, you are probably stuck with the package you started with, unless you are prepared to type in your stored records all over again.

Is the package available on a wide variety of computers, or only on a few highly esoteric systems? Packages which have been written for special purposes are sometimes available only on rarely-used computers or operating systems. This may make it hard to transfer to other packages or computers later. You may also be in particular difficulties if the supplier goes out of business.

Finally, the points in the sections which follow apply equally whether your solution is a special package or a general-purpose system. You still need to be concerned that the package has the detailed features you need, and is easy to use in your environment.

Data management systems versus integrated packages
Having decided that you need a more general approach to managing your information than a special-purpose package can provide, another consideration is the type of general-purpose system to choose. In most offices, you want to carry out a variety of tasks, some of which may share information, while others may be quite separate. In addition to the need to process structured information with which this book has been primarily concerned, you may also want to process letters and reports, using a word processor. Another increasingly popular application is the spreadsheet, in which you set up details about how your business is running at the moment, and project these figures by asking 'what-if' questions. You may also want to store information about appointments and meetings. If your system will be shared by several people, you may in addition want to communicate with others using the computer

rather than letter or telephone, via 'electronic mail'.

Some so-called 'integrated packages' are capable of carrying out all these tasks, while others are really a suite of packages with a common approach and some ability to share information between applications. As a broad general rule, the former approach tends to be more highly integrated, with less effort in switching between tasks, but with fewer features and above all considerable restrictions on the amount of information which can be handled. If you are considering such a system, the questions in the checklist on **quantities of information** will be particularly relevant. Those packages which take a 'family' approach, providing a suite of programs each with a different task, tend to be less well integrated, and for these the checklist on **communicating with other packages** will be especially relevant.

Where your needs are very precisely defined, and you are sure they are not likely to change, it may be best to purchase a special-purpose package aimed specifically at your application. You are most likely to get flexibility and room for change if you buy a package based on a data management system, rather than written in a programming language. If your requirements are very unusual, you may have to have a program written for you in this case too, you are likely to be better off with a tailored data management system rather than a program written in a language such as Basic. Were you to decide that you need a general-purpose data management system, you should also consider your other potential requirements, such as word processing. Whatever general approach you take, you should take into account the detailed points given in the checklists in the following Appendix.

Appendix of checklists: detailed features of data management systems

*This appendix contains a set of **checklists**, which summarise the points to look for in any package which can process structured information. These checklists are grouped in the same way as the material in Parts 1 to 3 of this book.*

Types of information and record structure (Chapters 2–4)
Data management systems fall into one of four general categories, distinguished by the kinds of information which can be handled, and the complexity of data structures provided. You will find it helpful to begin by deciding into which category your own needs fall. Within these categories, you should bear in mind the requirement that the package must be easy to use in your environment. As a general rule, the more complex the data structures which can be represented, the more difficult the package will be to use.

1 Does your information have a regular structure, with data which can be stored in a single set of records all of the same layout and size?
All data management systems can cope with this kind of information. The simplest (and cheapest) provide an 'automated card index', and have features appropriate to that approach. Virtually all the packages at the cheaper end of the market come into this category.

2 Do you need to include substantial amounts of text in your records, for instance in a library catalogue?
For this kind of information, you will need a package which provides similar features to those in the first category, but where the record structure is more flexible.

3   Are the components of your records related in a more complex way, so that you need to have some inter-relationship between sets of data?

If the different sets of records are related in a predictable and specific way, then you may be able to find a package which mirrors these relationships. For example, a data management system which uses a 'master-slave' ('transactional') approach would allow you to store one record for each patient in a doctor's practice plus one record for each consultation of a doctor by the patient.

4   Do you need complete flexibility to represent complex relationships among several sets of records?

Some data management systems on microcomputers come close to being true data base management systems. Like those systems in category 3, they provide for relationships among sets of data, but provide generalised facilities rather than being restricted to data related in any particular way.

In addition to the general question of structure, you should also consider some detailed points relating to the types of information that can be stored.

● What types of data can be represented?

Numbers, characters, dates may be essential, currency, yes/no types are useful. You should check:

Numbers
– representation of decimals
– maximum size of number and precision of digits
– ability to define fields which are calculated from other fields in the same record, and to choose when re-calculation takes place

Characters
– number allowed in one item
– ability to group like items (such as the lines of an address) together

Dates
– acceptable date format used
– calculations on dates performed correctly
– fields containing dates sorted correctly

- How does the package handle fields where the amount of information may vary considerably?
  If your records contain items with this characteristic, a system which uses an economical method of storing variable-length items will save you a lot of disk space.
- You may need to link sets of records with different structures together. If the package permits this, what linking methods are used? How many sets of record can be handled simultaneously? The most convenient systems allow you to define the relationships when the records are set up. For instance, you may store invoices and customer address records in separate files, each using the customer account number as a key. If you can tell the package that this relationship must exist, the records will be easier to check and to process.
- Does the package cater for records which have an irregular structure?

You may need to store information such as the list of members' interests in our club example.

Retrieving records (Chapters 6–8)
- Does the package allow you to retrieve records by entering the value of a particular field? If this direct access is permitted, you may need to check some subsidiary questions:

  - How large may the key field be?
  - Multiple keys – does the package permit direct access by several different fields? If it does, how many keys are allowed?
  - Are all the indexes kept up to date automatically?
  - Must the value in a key field be unique? Or may you require it to be unique?
  - Can you browse through a file after retrieving a record directly?

- What facilities are provided for retrieving records which match a set of criteria for selection?
- Can you specify the criteria and carry out the selection in one operation, or must the criteria be stored and then processed? Or may you optionally save the criteria for later re-use?

- What selection operators are allowed (equals, less than, not equals etc.)? Are special operators provided for fields which may contain letters (e.g. to check that a field **contains** a sequence of characters)? Are 'wild codes' available (e.g. * to match a group of characters or to match one character)?
- Does the package allow more than one test on a single field?
- How may criteria be combined? (You may want records that meet all tests, or any one, or some mix of combinations.)
- Does the package allow you to edit records which have been retrieved in this way, or may you only view them?
- Can you choose the order in which the records appear? How is this ordering achieved – by indexing, or by sorting? Can you have several levels of ordering, say town within county within country?

Displaying information (Chapter 9)

- Does the package provide a simple default format for screen layout?
- Can you design your own layout by 'painting' the format on the screen, or must you enter grid co-ordinates? Does the package show you the results of your design efforts as you progress?
- Can you design more than one layout for screen display? If so, is it possible to restrict this layout to part of each record? Can you attach a password to each layout to prevent unauthorised access?

Reporting (Chapter 10)

- Does the package provide a simple default format for reports?
- Can you design your own layout by 'painting' the report format on the screen, or must you enter grid co-ordinates? Does the package show you the results of your design efforts as you progress?
- Does the package calculate totals of numeric fields? If so, how easy is it to specify the positioning of these totals?
- Are sub-totals provided, and if so to how many levels? Is it the user's responsibility to ensure that the records are in the appropriate order before the report is printed?
- Can you request a report of summary information only?
- What kinds of summary can be provided (e.g. statistics such as

averages, counts of numbers of records)?
- Can you specify selection criteria to limit the report to a specific set of records? If so, can you use the same method as when selecting records for screen display?
- Can you display a report on the screen first, to check the layout. or to see summary information such as totals?

Communicating with other packages (Chapter 12)
- Can the package read and/or write records to a plain *ASCII* text file which can be used in conjunction with other packages?
- If this is possible, what formats are provided? Do these include the format required by your word processor or spreadsheet program?
- Does the package use a special disk format, which would preclude your keeping other types of files on the same disk (either at all, or except when expressly needed for communications)?

Quantities and speed (Chapter 13)
- Does the package perform well when processing large amounts of records (not just a demonstration set of 15 or 20 records)?
- Is the package quick to carry out tasks which involve interaction with the person using the system?
- What is the maximum number of records a file can contain? Is this the true limit, or are there other restrictions, such as the restriction on file size imposed by the operating system?
- Can a file span more than one disk? (If it cannot, a file will be limited to the size of a single disk.)
- What is the maximum number of characters a record may hold?
- What is the maximum number of fields permitted in a record?
- What is the maximum number of characters which can be stored in a character field?

Setting up and maintaining records (Chapters 14–16)
- Are you obliged to specify the maximum number of records the file is to contain?
- Does the package make it easy to ensure accuracy of information? What facilities are provided for data validation? Can you

echo a field value which is the same for a batch of records?
- Can you calculate field values from those of other fields, including constants in the calculation? If so, can you control the re-calculation of these fields? Can re-calculation be carried out for a group of records in a batch, without your intervention?
- Are the facilities for retrieving records for amendment flexible and easy to use?
- Can you set up several different screen formats for use in amending a single file, with password protection to ensure that only authorised users can see and amend sensitive information?
- Can the record definition be changed once data has been entered in the file? If so, can this be done without the need to copy the whole file, once or even twice?

Using the system (Chapters 17–18)
- How are instructions given to the package – by menus, commands, form-filling, question-and-answer?
- Can the package be tailored to individual needs, and to what extent? Is there an interface to a programming language if needed?
- Does the package come with a tutorial guide, reference manual, reference summary, and 'cookbook' or 'How Do I . . .' guide? Are these manuals clear, well laid out, and comprehensive without being formidably large?

Sharing information (Chapter 19)
- Can the system be shared by several people at a time? If so, what mechanism is used to ensure that users needing access to the same record do not interfere with one another?

Sources of supply and training (Chapters 20–21)
- Does the supplier provide training? What does it cost? Are there alternative sources of training?
- Does the supplier or the manufacturer provide telephone support? At what cost?
- Is there a user group? How active is it, and what is the subscription?
- Do you know of other people nearby who use the package, and could help you to get started?

Further information

Initial help can be gained from the popular computing magazines such as *Personal Computer World* and the machine specific publications such as *16-Bit Computing* and *PC User*. For larger systems, *Which Computer?* may help.

Individual advice is available from the *NCC Microcomputer Systems Advisory Centres*, and (where appropriate) from the *Small Firms Advisory Service*; addresses should be in your phone book.

Many local colleges run good courses on using computers, or there are several companies which specialise in training who advertise nationally in the magazines.

Finally, for a fee, you can get help from consultants: the *British Computer Society* has a register. But do check that they have fully declared their interests, if any, in the systems they recommend.

Information at work: Glossary

ASCII
A method of coding characters in binary form, used by most microcomputers.

Acoustic hood
Device to reduce noise emitted by printers. Usually essential for daisy-wheel printers in shared offices.

Benchmark
Test of performance, either of the computer system or of a package running on a computer system.

Bug
Error in a computer system.

Call-out
Time taken by maintenance engineer to come to mend your computer. Usually a maximum call-out is written into a maintenance contract.

Comma-delimited format
Form of record used by many programs, especially as a transport format and for mail-merge applications. Consists of each field in a record separated by a comma, with the record terminated by a carriage-return character.

Command
Explicit unprompted instruction given by the user to a package or to the computer system.

182

Consumables
Items such as paper, floppy disks and printer ribbons which must be purchased for
the computer.

DIF format
Format used to store records in spreadsheet packages. DIF is trade mark of Software
Arts who produced it.

Daisy-wheel
Light interchangeable wheel with letters, numbers and symbols mounted on spokes.
Used to produce typewriter-quality text on an appropriate computer printer.

Data
Information, commonly information stored in a computer.

Data base management system
Suite of programs for handling a data base (a set of files all linked together through a
common data dictionary).

Data management system
Package for handling structured records, either in single file or in several related
files. User must be fully aware of record formats and must usually maintain relationships between files explicitly.

Debug
Detection of an error in a computer system.

Default
Value given to a field or option if no explicit value is assigned.

Documentation
Written information describing the working of part of the computer system.

Dot-matrix
Series of dots used to build up characters, produced by computer printers which are

usually smaller, cheaper and often more reliable than daisy-wheel printers, but usually produce output of lower quality.

Field
A single item, such as a member's name or phone number. Several items are stored together in a record.

File
A collection of records all having the same format and containing the same number of items.

File locking
Where a system cannot perform record locking, it may use file locking instead. Usually this is less satisfactory, as the file may be unavailable for long periods if a user is making many changes.

Flat file
A file stored on a computer system in which every record has the same structure, in contrast to a data base.

Form-filling
Display of set of options on the screen as a form which the user can fill in by moving the cursor to each option in turn and entering the desired response.

Index
Set of pointers to show how records should be ordered by a key.

Installation
A complete computer system with its associated printer(s) and software.

Internal format
Form of records held internally by a data management system. Usually records stored in this way cannot be displayed except within that system.

Key
One or more fields in a record which have been nominated to be used regularly to

gain access to the record. Most data management packages have ways of giving fast access to records using one or more keys.

Maintenance
Servicing and mending the computer or its software. Usually carried out under contract by supplier.

Many-to-many relationship
Relation between two sets of information in which multiple links may exist between records in each set, e.g. products and suppliers, where a supplier may provide several products, and for each product there may be several sources of supply.

Menu
A list of options from which the user may select one.

Mnemonic
Name or word whose meaning is easily remembered, e.g. calling the field which will hold a person's surname 'Name' reminds you what the field will contain.

Multi-user
A facility which can be used by several people at the same time.

One-to-many relationship
Relation between one set of information and another, where a single record in one set (e.g. a patient's personal details) relates to many records in another set (e.g. one record for each consultation the patient has with a doctor).

Paint-a-screen
Method of setting out a screen format by moving the cursor to places where fields are to be positioned.

Posting
Transferring records from one file (usually the file in which transactions have been entered, such as a batch of invoices) to others where the data is to be stored (e.g. to sales and nominal ledgers).

Question-and-answer
Method by which a package extracts instructions from the user by asking questions
and recording the answers.

Record
A set of closely related items of information stored together, e.g. the details of a
particular club member's name, address, etc.

Record locking
When a file can be changed by several people at once in a multi-user system, the
system must be able to lock the record so that only the first person who tries to make a
change can do so. Others may still be able to view the record.

Screen dump
Direct copy of the information displayed on the terminal screen, sent for printing.

Screen format
Layout of information on the terminal screen, file containing a record of such a
format.

Selection criteria
Set of tests to determine whether a record should be extracted for printing or display.

Sequential access
Retrieval of records by reading each record in turn rather than retrieving individual
records directly.

Sheet-feeder
Device which permits automatic feeding of single sheets of paper to a computer
printer.

Spike
Electrical surge which may cause loss of information on the computer system's
storage.

Surprise, Principle of Minimum
Rule that a program should behave in a consistent way, so that the user can infer its method of working in one area from its method in another.

Transaction processing
Processing of many records which are batched together, often to be linked up to existing records as in the master/transaction relationship.

Transport format
Format used to pass records between computer programs which use different internal formats.

User image
The image of the computer system or of a package as experienced by the user when carrying out tasks. A system which is easy and convenient to use is often called 'user-friendly'.

Wild code
Code used in a test which will match any character (or sometimes any sequence of characters). Works like a joker in Canasta.

Acknowledgement

The author gratefully acknowledges permission to use the following trade marks in *Data Management at Work*:

Busifile, Urmbeta Systems, Southport
Cardbox Caxton Software, London
Condor Granite Chip Microsystems, Aberdeen
dBASE II, Ashton Kate, Milton Keynes
Delta Composoft, Guildford
Everyman, Vector Systems International, London
Pearl, Genesis Ltd, London
Resumé, Grade One, Glossop
Tomorrow's Office, Sosoft, Poole, Dorset

Index